Connecticut Attacked: A British Viewpoint,

Tryon's Raid on Danbury

By ROBERT F. McDEVITT

Globe
Pequot

Guilford, Connecticut

Published by Globe Pequot
An imprint of The Rowman & Littlefield Publishing Group, Inc.
4501 Forbes Boulevard, Suite 200, Lanham, Maryland 20706
www.rowman.com

Unit A, Whitacre Mews, 26-34 Stannary Street, London SE11 4AB

Distributed by NATIONAL BOOK NETWORK

British Library Cataloguing in Publication Information Available

Library of Congress Cataloging-in-Publication Data
The first paperback edition of this book was previously cataloged by the Library of
Congress as follows:

ISBN: 87106-050-7
Library of Congress Catalog Card Number: 74-82315

ISBN 978-0-87106-050-1 (paper : alk. paper)
ISBN 978-1-49303-309-6 (electronic)

♾️ The paper used in this publication meets the minimum requirements of
American National Standard for Information Sciences—Permanence of Paper for
Printed Library Materials, ANSI/NISO Z39.48-1992.

Printed in the United States of America

Contents

Preface

THE first two years of the *Revolutionary War* were largely years of frustration and defeat for the hastily-organized American Army. How that army was brought into being in the months following the battle of Concord is another story. Suffice it to say that it is remarkable that the problems of recruitment, organization, and supply were overcome to the degree that they were. Somehow an army was forged, and it besieged the British forces, confined at first, largely, to Boston proper.

The Americans, lacking heavy artillery and ammunition, dared not attempt to dislodge the British from their secure defensive positions. The British, on their part, made no attempt to break out of the encircling ring of raw Colonial troops led by George Washington whose military experience had been limited to that of Colonel of Militia in the French and Indian War.

Sir William Howe, having assumed command of the British army from General Thomas Gage, simply evacuated Boston. He chose New York City as his main base from which he confidently expected to subdue the rebels. A series of battles and skirmishes won the city for the British. Only Howe's inexplicable lack of persistence, with total victory in his grasp, allowed Washington's army to remain intact and capable of continued resistance.

These first battles of the war clearly showed the weaknesses of the Americans, as they pitted themselves against a well-equipped and thoroughly-trained professional army. Poor battlefield tactics, lack of a unified command, inexperienced levies of militia, and shortages of war materiel proved to be obstacles that nearly defeated the American cause. Most of these problems, in varying degrees, account for the British success in destroying the magazines at Danbury, Connecticut, April 26-28, 1777.

Operating from his secure base at New York, Howe swept the hapless Continentals before him as he cleared New Jersey of all opposition. With their backs to the Delaware and the army all but decimated, Washington and his meager forces were saved from final defeat only by the onset of winter and the traditional winter cessation of hostilities. Howe went into winter quarters, secure in the knowledge that the spring and summer of 1777 would bring him final victory. So secure was he in his belief that the rebellion was all but over that, as early as November 27, 1776, he dispatched General Henry Clinton with a force of about 6,000 men to take and hold Newport, Rhode Island, this to serve as a base from which to subdue New England in the spring of 1777. Cornwallis had been granted leave to return to England; spring would be soon enough to destroy the collapsing American cause.

Howe's assessment of American prospects for success was probably quite correct. December, 1776, found the American cause at its lowest point. A year of successive defeats in the field had seriously impaired morale and enthusiasm. Shortage of necessary equipment, clothes and food were ever present, as was the specter of an army simply evaporating through desertion and the expiration of short-term enlistments.

Realizing that something dramatic was needed to electrify the country in order to hold the army together, Washington planned a bold stroke against several of the isolated and exposed posts held by the British, in early December. If successful, this might serve to inspire the army and aid in the recruitment of the additional forces needed to meet the challenge of the spring.

With all to gain and nothing to lose, Washington executed a brilliant and daring thrust at two of these exposed positions, Trenton and Princeton. In both battles, the ragged and weary Continentals won surprising victories over the Hessian and British troops. Between December 25, 1776, and January 6, 1777, some eleven days, the British were swept from western and central New Jersey. The only positions still in their hands were New Brunswick and Amboy.

As the Americans went into winter quarters at Morristown, New Jersey, Washington had the satisfaction of knowing that the cause had been saved and that there would be an American force in the field next spring. To the men had come the realization that, in Washington, they had a commander equal to the enemy's best.

In spite of their recent setbacks, the British were supremely confident that the spring of 1777 would see the end of the conflict. General Clinton, who had taken Newport, Rhode Island, would move out to subdue New England, while General Howe would move against Philadelphia. General Burgoyne, acting under orders from Lord Germain, was to move down from Canada. His objective would be to gain control of the Hudson, thereby splitting the rebellious colonies in two. Oddly enough, both Howe and Burgoyne were given Lord Germain's blessing for their separate enterprises, and there was apparently no effort to coordinate these two forces. Such were the British plans for the coming spring of 1777.

These events determined, to a large degree, the courses of action that both the Americans and British followed with regard to the raid on Danbury, Connecticut, in April of 1777. In many respects, the disposition of opposing forces, as determined by the closing weeks of 1776, affected the strategy of both armies and their commanders with regard to the raid. These circumstances also determined the ultimate outcome of the British raid to destroy the magazine of stores kept at Danbury, Connecticut.

6

The Causes of and Contributory Factors to the British Raid on Danbury

The Strategies of the Two Armies

WASHINGTON'S DILEMMA

The victories at Trenton and Princeton had saved the day for the American cause. New levies were being raised by the states, and they were beginning to swell the ranks of Washington's army wintering in New Jersey. The Commander-in-Chief's concern over the complete collapse of the American cause was, at least for the present, put aside while he pondered an old and more immediate problem. It was essentially the same problem he had faced one year before: What would be Howe's main objective in the forthcoming spring campaign?

As a result of the reverses suffered in the closing weeks of 1776, Howe was restricted to his main base in North America (New York), except for Amboy and New Brunswick in New Jersey, and a force of 6,000 sent to Newport, Rhode Island (November 27, 1776), under Clinton.[1] British control of the sea and the huge armada of 260-odd ships under the command of Admiral Richard Howe[2] gave Sir William Howe the option of striking when and where he chose. As Washington himself expressed it, "The amazing advantage the enemy derives from their ships and the command of the water keeps us in a state of constant perplexity and the most anxious conjecture."[3] This was Washington's problem: would Howe move up the Hudson, using his naval strength to force the American defensive position in the Highlands? Would this be part of a co-ordinated British move from Canada? Perhaps New England would be the main objective in the spring campaign, with Howe striking Boston as part of a concerted drive with Sir Henry Clinton based upon Rhode Island. Or maybe Howe's efforts were to be further south? Philadelphia? Charleston? Any one of these objectives, or combination thereof, was entirely possible, as the land force depended upon the water, and the water was controlled by the British navy.[4] Such was the problem faced by Washington in the spring of 1777. With a relatively small nucleus of Continentals and a larger but unpredictable force of militia, Washington had to meet any one of several possible thrusts. How Washington chose to utilize his meager force was to have a direct bearing upon later events in Danbury.

Following his successful assault on Fort Washington in November, 1776, and continuing through March, 1777, Howe formulated and sent to Lord Germain for approval three separate plans for the campaign of 1777.[5] He apparently realized that the rebellion could not be quelled in the remaining months of 1776.

His first plan (November, 1776) was the most ambitious, and was based on the assumption that Lord Germain could and would meet his request for 15,000 additional troops. With these reinforcements, Howe planned to launch three simultaneous offensives: (1) into New England, (2) into New Jersey, and (3) up the Hudson. The move into New Jersey with 8,000 men was to be the smallest, and, in Howe's own words, intended "to keep General Washington's army in check, by giving a jealousy to Philadelphia, which as well as Virginia, I propose to attack in autumn provided the success of other operations should have admitted of sending thither an adequate force."[6]

In a letter to Lord Germain, dated December 20, 1776,[7] General Howe proposed a second plan based on the assumption that the people of Pennsylvania seemed to be "disposed to peace" as a result of the "late progress of the army." (This was prior to the January, 1777, defeats of Trenton and Princeton.) Howe further stated: "I am from this consideration fully persuaded the principal Army should act offensively on that side, where the enemy's chief strength will certainly be collected." By this plan, New England would have to be deferred until the reinforcements arrived from Europe. A corps might be provided to act defensively upon the lower Hudson, protect his flank, "as well as to facilitate, in some degree, the approach of the army from Canada."[8]

Upon receipt of a letter from the Secretary of State, dated January 14, 1777, and received March 9, which stated that he was not to expect any reinforcements, Howe stated to a committee of the House of Commons, April 29: "I relinquished . . . the idea of any offensive operation, except to the Southward, and a *diversion occasionally upon Hudson's River or to enter Connecticut as circumstances may point out.*"[9]

This, then, was Howe's third and final plan for the campaign of 1777. He would leave 4,700 men in New York City, 2,400 in Rhode Island. Governor William Tryon was placed in command of 3,000 Tories in the vicinity of his principal base, and this force would be used as the diversion upon the Hudson or in Connecticut.[10]

While Howe was in New York formulating his plans for the forth-coming campaign, General John Burgoyne was back in England where, in February, he submitted his plan to Germain for a three-pronged attack to isolate New England.[11] The plan was an old one: it consisted of moving down from Canada with three forces by means of the waterways, then to effect a junction with a fourth force moving northward from New York, the objective being to split the rebellious colonies in two. This plan, like Howe's, was approved by both Lord Germain and King George.[12]

William B. Wilcox sums up the situation concisely, in *Portrait of a General* (Sir Henry Clinton):

> The planning of the Campaign of 1777 was the worst that the British perpetrated throughout the war. Their strategy in the Yorktown campaign, four years later, was even more disastrous in its outcome but far more defensible in its design. The strategy of 1777 can scarcely be defended at all. It had no unifying concept, and it rested upon a wildly fallacious premise—that the main field army could safely operate in Pennsylvania, while a substantial garrison was immobilized on Manhattan and Burgoyne was left to his own devices in the north. Each of these three British armies was isolated from the other two, and the Americans were free to concentrate against whichever one they chose. The absurdity of dispersing forces in this way was apparent to Clinton in April if not before. Why was it not equally apparent to Germain and Howe and Burgoyne? Or even to the King, who had considerable common sense? The question, like that of why the Howes squandered their opportunities in 1776, has been endlessly debated; and again no final answer is possible. But an examination of the men who were principally responsible, Germain and Burgoyne and Howe, suggests that two major factors were at work. One was the intellectual shortcomings of the three architects; the other was an almost complete lack of communication between them.[13]

As a result of poor communication, a divided command in North America since the recall of General Gage,[14] and the characters, personalities, and abilities of the principals concerned, the British were to place two armies in the field acting independently of one another, while a third force was to remain immobilized in a defensive posture at New York City and a fourth force (Clinton's) was to remain totally inactive in Rhode Island.

The scene, then, was set. All that remained was to fill in the specific reasons and contributory factors that led to Howe's decision to attack the rebel military supply depot at Danbury.

One factor that must certainly be taken into consideration was Washington's strategy as he pondered the question of where Howe intended to strike. Intelligence received from spies and deserters informed Washington that the British were enlarging their base in New Brunswick and were building a large portable bridge that could be transported on wagons.[15] This could mean only one thing: an overland thrust through New Jersey, a crossing of the Delaware, and an assault on Philadelphia, the seat of the Continental Congress. Congress had since returned from Baltimore, where it had fled when Howe endangered Philadelphia in the closing months of 1776. Congress made it clear to Washington that he must devote adequate attention to the defense of the capital.[16]

Washington's sources also informed him that a vast fleet of warships and transports was being assembled in New York Harbor, obviously to support an expedition by water.[17] Would this be a thrust up the Hudson to form a junction with Burgoyne's force from the north?

In order to be ready to meet either of these two possibilities, Washington decided to maintain his position in New Jersey with his main army, while continuing to hold the Hudson Highlands defensive complex with a lesser force. This force, under General Heath, continued to be based upon Peekskill, New York. With this plan, Washington hoped to be in a position to defend either of the two possible British objectives by moving the main American force across New Jersey to a site between Howe and his objective. Washington could not, of course, commit his modest force until British intentions were well defined.

WASHINGTON REINFORCES HIS MAIN ARMY

To bring his strength in New Jersey to the optimum, Washington requested that all available units being raised in New England be forwarded to his command with all possible dispatch. In effect, he was draining Connecticut and Massacuhsetts of manpower to bolster his force operating in New Jersey.

The urgency of Washington's request for men is reflected in the exchange of letters between the Commander-in-Chief and the field officers under his command in the Peekskill-Western Connecticut area. On December 21, 1776, Washington wrote to General Alexander McDougall: "I have ordered General Heath to join me with as many of the Connecticut and Massachusetts militia as can be spared."[18]

Six days later, Washington wrote to General William Heath: "I must request you will forward the militia with all expedition."[19]

Benedict Arnold also wrote to Heath, from Fishkill, New York, on December 28, 1776: "I have received express orders from General Washington to forward on the Militia from Massachusetts and Connecticut as fast as possible to Headquarters." Arnold added: "I have the pleasure to hear this minute that a large number of the Militia are arrived at Peek's Kills. I may not doubt you will forward them on as fast as possible."[20]

General Heath replied to Washington on December 28, 1776: "If the Eastern Militia should arrive, agreeable to your Excellency's expectations, I shall without loss of time move forward with them to join your Excellency."[21]

From General Jonathon Warner, Commander at Danbury, came a letter to General Heath dated December 28, 1776: "Agreeable to request, I have ordered one regiment to march this morning from Peekskill."[22] And, incredibly, as late as April 26, Colonel Jeddediah Huntington wrote that he was forwarding forty or fifty Connecticut men, "—one-half of all that are here present," to Peekskill.[23]

Washington's strategy thus had the effect of laying western Connecticut open to attack. This did not go unnoticed, as evidenced by an almost prophetic letter written by General David Wooster to Governor Jonathon Trumbull of Connecticut, dated January 9, 1777: "It is not a little surprising to me that General Heath should expect the Connecticut Militia to Rendevouse [sic] at the Peekskills and leave all the western part of Connecticut to the ravages and rapine of worse than a savage enemy."[24] Wooster's fears were to come true, as the Danbury undertaking was, indeed, a move into western Connecticut, and he was to die defending his state.

HOWE'S GESTURE TO BURGOYNE

A second contributing factor leading to the attack on Danbury was Howe's final plan for 1777. Having received only a fraction of the reinforcements he had requested, 2,900 men in all, with 1,700 more to arrive in September,[25] Howe decided that Philadelphia and Washington's main army should be his principal concern. The best that he could promise for Burgoyne was "the diversions on the Hudson and into Connecticut." Thus, it is entirely possible that the British raid on Peekskill, New York, on March 23, 1777, under the command of Colonel Bird,[26] and the raid on Danbury, Connecticut, one month later, were, in part, gestures of assistance to Burgoyne. Of course, any offensive move by Howe into the Hudson River-Connecticut area could be considered advantageous to the British commander, in that it might serve to decoy Washington away from Howe's primary target—Philadelphia.

Howe has been severely criticized by historians for the lateness with which he opened the campaign of 1777, the usual explanation being laid to his sluggish temperament and his adherence to the classic tradition that winter was a time to be spent in quarters, not in the field.[27] In fairness to Howe, however, it should be noted that his reinforcements, such as they were, did not arrive until late in the season, and the equipment he needed for the forthcoming campaign did not arrive until May 24, 1777.[28] While his entire force was in need of these supplies, the German mercenaries under his command were extremely short of supplies. The German princes were not in the habit of sending their men well-equipped.[29] In his letter to Lord Germain, dated December 20, 1776, Howe stated: "Clothing, tents, and every species of camp equipment will be wanted for the Hession troops and regiment of Waldeck."[30] Circumstaances over which he had little control dictated Howe's timetable. Until he could be resupplied from England, he was forced to remain immobile at New York. Also, the reverses in the closing weeks of 1776 had the effect of putting Howe in a state of siege,[31] similar, in some respects, to Gage's position in Boston following Concord and Lexington.

It had been a most difficult winter for the British in the New York City-Amboy-New Brunswick area. Housing for the troops in New York City was very scarce as a result of several fires that destroyed many of the existing structures. The largest of these fires, which raged for two days, broke out on September 20, 1776.[32] Howe assumed this to be sabotage on Washington's part, although no proof appears to exist. There had been a controversy between Washington and his staff as to whether New York City should be burned, but the decision, based upon orders from Congress, was that no damage should be done to it.[33]

Howe's 13,000 men in New Brunswick and Amboy, and his 10,000 additional troops in New York, suffered much discomfort as a result of the housing shortage. In Amboy and New Brunswich, entire companies were housed in two rooms, with churches housing regiments. Stables and sheds were pressed into service. Many of the troops were forced to lie in the open.[34]

The countryside, too, was unable to supply much in the way of food.[35] From the end of the campaign of 1776 until they took the field in June of 1777, foraging for food became the British Army's principal occupation.[36]

These foraging parties were constantly harassed by American troops, notably the New Jersey Militia. As the Americans suffered at Morristown for want of fuel, clothing, and shelter, so did their British counterparts at New York, New Brunswich, and Amboy.[37]

A third consideration, then, of Howe's decision to attack both Peekskill and Danbury was the need to obtain food for his troops, confined as they were to an area unable to sustain them. What is now Westchester County was a bitterly-contested area for forage and plunder, and, by the spring of 1777, largely picked clean. This area, known as "the Neutral Ground," ran south to New York City from a line roughly drawn from New Rochelle to Phillipse Manor; at other times the line ran to the north side of the Croton River.[38]

THE RAID ON PEEKSKILL, NEW YORK

Howe had been told by men in his service that a store of supplies was maintained at Peekskill, and Colonel Beverly Robinson of the Loyal Americans (Tories) and one Captain Pemart, a Tory sloop captain doing business between Peekskill and New York, supplied Howe with the information he needed to launch an attack.[39] As a result of the raid on Peekskill, large quantities of military stores were destroyed, and forty sheep in addition to eight or ten head of cattle were carried off by Colonel Bird and his men.[40] It seems clear that this raid and the raid on Danbury a month later were designed, in part, as foraging expeditions.

A final item of concern to Howe, one which undoubtedly affected the timing of the spring offensive, was the shortage of hay and oats for his horses. Despite his requests for these items, London failed to send sufficient amounts, forcing him to wait until green forage was on the ground.[41]

PERSONALITY AND MOTIVES OF TRYON

Any listing of the causes and contributing factors with regard to the raid on Danbury would not be complete without consideration of the motives and personality of one of its chief participants, the man who was to lead the expedition, General William Tryon.

As Governor of North Carolina, Tryon had earned for himself a reputation for sternness in the quelling of a backcountry rebellion. A group of citizens, which called itself the Regulators, revolted against the imposition of illegal fees and excessive taxes collected by dishonest officials appointed by Governor Tryon.[42] With a force of 1,018 militia infantry and thirty light horse, Tryon marched against this group of half-armed and completely unorganized citizenry (May, 1771). In the rout that followed, homes and farms were ravaged and looted. Those who survived were forced, under duress, to take an oath of allegiance to the king and to swear "never to bear arms against the King, but to take up arms for him, if called upon."[43] Such was the reputation that preceded Lord Tryon to New York.

Prior to his appointment as Lieutenant Governor of North Carolina in 1764 (acceding to the governorship one year later upon the death of Governor Dobbs), Tryon had had a distinguished career in the British army. Arriving in New York, Tryon found that British control did not extend beyond New York City, which, for all practical purposes, was an armed military camp.[44] After November of 1776, there was no civil authority from Nova Scotia to Florida.[45] As governor, he performed a limited but useful service to the Crown by means of his correspondence with certain Tories, and in the organization of Tory military units.[46] His prior military service apparently made his civil duties appear dull by comparison, as he applied for active duty and was soon commissioned a Major General of Provincials. Charles Stedman, the commissary officer to General Howe, who later was to write a two-volume history of the war, stated that Tryon "panted for a military command."[47] This strong inclination to get back into uniform and strike a blow is borne out in Tryon's own words in a letter to Lord Germain, dated December 31, 1776:

My Lord: Last Sunday evening Mr. Wallace and Mr. Jauncey, two of his Majesty's Council of this Province, with several other inhabitants thereof, came to town from Connecticut, having been discharged by Governour Trumbull from their confinement upon the express obligation of not taking up arms against America, and to return to their captivity if required. By these gentlemen I understand the temper of the warmest patriots in Connecticut is much softened, and that they wish for peace; they also tell me, from the intelligence they had opportunities to collect, they are positive a majority of the inhabitants of Connecticut river are firm friends of Government. This report I can give the more credit to, from the number of Connecticut men that inlist in the Provincial corps now raising.

The Rebels carrying off the Hessian brigade under Colonel Rall, at Trenton, has given me more real chagrin than any other circumstance this war. The moment was critical, and I believe the Rebel chiefs were conscious if some stroke was not struck that would give life to their sinking cause, they should not raise another army. Unlucky as was this loss, I have received great comfort by the assurance General Heister and General Kniphausen have given me, (who are most sincerely and deeply mortified at the event), that the Rebels will not, with all their arts, be able to seduce the Hessian prisoners from their allegiance to their Prince and duty to his Majesty. I trust this tarnish to the campaign, will in due season be wiped away by some brilliant enterprise of the King's forces, who entertain the keenest sense of the insult.

I am, with all possible respect, my Lord, your Lordship's most obedient, and very humble servant, Wm. Tryon.[48]

A final factor that undoubtedly influenced the thinking of Tryon, and therefore may have had an indirect influence on Howe, was Tryon's estimate of Tory influence and the morale of the rebels in Connecticut. In his letter to Germain of December 31, 1776, Tryon had stated that "the temper of the warmest patriots in Connecticut is much softened and that they wish for peace," and that "a majority of the inhabitants of Connecticut river are firm friends of Government." To what degree this estimate of rebel morale and Tory strength influenced Tryon and Howe in their thoughts concerning the raid on Danbury and, in a larger sense, all of western Connecticut, is difficult to ascertain. Those responsible for British strategy seemed to have grievously overestimated the number of rebels disenchanted with their cause. Their estimate seemed to indicate that only the appearance of the King's forces was needed to put an end to this unfortunate incident. By this reasoning, the loyal subjects of the Crown could openly declare their allegiance, while the majority of the rebels, doubting the wisdom of taking up arms and disheartened by reverses, would flock back to the fold. The few remaining die-hards would be easy to handle. This estimate was not without some foundation. The Howe brothers had arrived in America as military commanders and as peace negotiators, bearing the King's commission "for restoring peace to his Majesty's Colonies and Plantations in North America." A proclamation issued by the Admiral and Sir William offered a "free and general pardon" to all who would return to "their just allegiance." The Howes scored considerable success with this proclamation in New Jersey, where the populace seemed to be most interested in being on the winning side.[49] It was only the excesses of the British and German forces in their treatment of civilians that largely nullified these early successes.

We might recall that one of Howe's main points in support of his plans to advance into Pennsylvania was his contention that the people of Pennsylvania were "disposed to peace." It is not wholly inconceivable, then, that by means of his own intelligence or information supplied to him by Tryon, Howe reasoned that a British display of arms might produce a valuable political victory in Connecticut in much the same manner as he had planned for Pennsylvania.

Another consideration favoring some action, indeed *any* action, by Howe in the spring of 1777 was the mounting wave of criticism over his failure to produce a final victory in 1776 and his apparent indolence as the spring of 1777 drew near.[50]

CONCLUSION OF BRITISH MOTIVES

Thus, it appears likely that the decision to send a large British force deep into rebel territory goes beyond the simple theory that it is

15

sound military strategy to deny your enemy the materiel of war.

We find the British forces confined to a limited area and forced into idleness by the tardy arrival of men and supplies. The need for food, fuel and fodder was a pressing one. So, too, was the need to counter the dissatisfaction from among Loyalist elements in America and from England regarding the lateness with which the spring campaign was beginning. Howe also had the problem of how to assist Burgoyne as he came south from Canada. Howe was not under specific orders to help this force, nor did he even feel a moral obligation to give more than token aid to Burgoyne who answered only to Lord Germain. His statements on this matter clearly indicated that he might aid Burgoyne only in a limited divisionary sense.

Other factors tipping the scales in favor of an expedition into Connecticut were the motives and the attitude of Tryon, and his influence on General Howe. An expedition of this nature would, according to Tryon, be fruitful in a political sense in that a large segment of Americans would be returned to their proper allegiance.

Since Washington had drawn large numbers of men from western Connecticut to New Jersey, the way was open to strike this region with relative impunity. Howe, having received intelligence that sizeable amounts of enemy stores were kept at Danbury, which was, for all practical purposes, unprotected, decided that here was a most opportune target. In retrospect, a more desirable target could not have been chosen. The expedition against Danbury in April, 1777, would meet any one or all of the considerations facing Howe.

The Organization and Composition of the British Expeditionary Force

INTELLIGENCE RECEIVED BY HOWE

News that a "large magazine of military stores and provisions" had been collected at Danbury reached General Howe in New York some time in early April, this intelligence having been collected by an agent who had been sent by Colonel Guy Johnson on a vast sweep through upper New York State to ascertain the strengths of rebel garrisons. Johnson's letter of June 8, 1777, to Lord Germain, while postdating the raid, provides us with the first evidence of the impending event and an approximation of the date on which the information was received.

My Lord,

   In my letter of April last I mentioned briefly the state of matters at that time; a few days after a person whom I employed to carry messages to the Indians and obtain an account of the rebel garrisons returned, with a full state of the strength and circumstances of the Forts from Ticonderoga to Albany, which he obtained thro' his address under an assumed character, *and likewise gave a particular account of a large magazine of military stores and provisions collected at Danbury in Connecticut: which I communicated to Sr Wm Howe, who soon after sent a body of troops there, that effectually destroyed the whole, as he has doubtless acquainted your Lordship. . . .*[1]

The bearer of the above intelligence might be partially identified in an earlier communication of November 25, 1776, from Johnson to Germain.

   . . . I have, with the approbation of General Howe, lately dispatched (in disguise) one of my officers with Joseph the Indian Chief (who desired the Service) to get across the country to the Six Nations.[2]

Should the unidentified officer mentioned in the letter of November 25, 1776, and the person traveling under an assumed character mentioned in the letter of June 8, 1777, be one and the same, we might, then, conclude that the forces culminating in the raid itself were set in motion sometime prior to November 25, 1776.

There appears to be no written communication between Johnson and Howe on the subject of the stores at Danbury. Johnson was in New York City at this time, acting in his capacity as Superintendent of Indian Affairs. His alleged purpose was to co-ordinate operations of the main British Army with those of the Indians and Tories of upper New York State and Canada. But, like many prominent Loyalists, he served as a clearinghouse for information that ultimately found its way to British military headquarters.[3]

It would seem most probable that Johnson, in view of his official capacity and influence, had direct access to Sir William Howe at British headquarters in New York City, and that the information collected by Johnson was orally transmitted to Howe.

Upon receipt of this most opportune intelligence, Howe appears to have moved with alacrity. Here was a target that could meet one or all of the considerations pressing the British Commander-in-Chief. At the very least, an expedition to destroy enemy stores would serve to allay the mounting criticism of his inaction.

Howe, in his last campaign plan submitted to London on April 2, had intended to utilize Governor Tryon and a force of 3,000 Tories in a diversionary effort "upon the Hudson or for use in Connecticut." This correspondence (April 2) must have been dispatched about the time of receipt of Johnson's intelligence. Here, then, was a happy coincidence and opportunity, too good for Howe to let pass.

Orders, emanating from British army headquarters in New York City and Admiral Howe's flagship, give us a clear picture of the formation of the striking force, its composition, and proposed means of transport:

> Head Quarters, New York, April 20th, 1777
>
> Governor Tryon having been pleased to offer his Services to Command the Provincial Troops in this Province, is appointed to that Command, with the Rank of Major Gen^L. of Provincial Forces, and is to be obeyed as such.
>
> Captn Wemyss of the 40th Reg^t is appointed Aid [sic] de Camp to Maj^r Genl Tryon, and is to be observed as such.
>
> Lieu^t Bird 16th Reg^t is appointed Supernumerary Aid [sic] de Camp to Major Genl Tryon, and is to be observed as such.[4]

This offer to command the Provincial troops was made by Tryon to Lord Howe early in February, 1777, as evidenced by the following communication from Tryon to Lord Germain:

> New York   12 Feb. 1777
>
> I waited upon Gen. Howe last week to offer my services to command the provincials in the ensuing campaign, if he would make the proper and creditable appointments for that corps and give me an establishment, suitable to the situation His Mag^ty has placed me in here [Governor of New York].
>
> Sir Wm. Howe was pleased to approve the proposition, but has not as yet appointed the staff, or other arrangements for that command.[5]

On April 2, 1777, Lord Germain wrote to Tryon that the proposition had the full approval of the Crown:

> I received from General Sir William Howe that he intended accepting the offer you made of your services to command the loyal American levies, and I have the honor to signify to the General His Maj. approbation of that intention.[6]

As Tryon applied to Howe for command two months before the intelligence reached New York concerning the stores kept at Danbury, he could not have been motivated personally towards the citizens of Danbury, as many accounts would have us believe. In all probability Tryon's request for command was occasioned by his eagerness to strike a blow in retaliation for the stinging losses suffered by British forces in New Jersey during the closing days of 1776.

It must be remembered, also, that Tryon had had a distinguished military career before his appointments to the governorships of North Carolina and New York. With all civil government suspended, Tryon's inaction as a civil administrator must have been galling. His request for command can be viewed simply as an old soldier's eagerness to return to active duty.

18

The following order from British army headquarters clearly places Tryon at the head of the expedition already formed and embarked:

Head Quarters, 22[d] April, 1777

Major Gen[l] Tryon is appointed to Command the Troops, embarked this day upon an Expedition; All reports to be made to him, and all Troops ordered to join that Armament, will put themselves under his Command.[7]

CHRONOLOGY OF EVENTS

It appears certain that the orders to the regiments that were to participate in the expedition had been issued sometime prior to the 21st of April. By that date, the troops had been embarked and awaited shipping in the North River (Hudson River). Colonel Stephen Kemble, Deputy Adjutant General to Howe, recorded in his journal:

Monday—April 21st   The 4th, 15th, 23rd, 27th, 44th, and 64th Regiments, two hundred men each, Embarked about three or four in the Afternoon, in the Vessels prepared for their reception in the North River, and were to have sailed immediately, but the tide being far spent before they were on board, their sailing till tomorrow.[8]

Captain Archibald Robertson, the British Engineer Officer who accompanied the expedition to Danbury, made this terse entry in his Diary for April 21st: "—the men were embarked."[9]

We may never be able to establish a specific date or throw much light on the early stages of the operation, as the complete headquarters papers of General Howe, while Commander-in-Chief (1775-1778), are believed to have been destroyed by fire in Ireland.[10] Those that have survived have been culled from the papers of Germain and Tryon, orderly books, and like sources. Lacking documentary evidence on this point, any date picked as marking the start of the expedition must be largely conjectural. From supportive evidence, however, it is reasonable to assume that the planning and logistics necessary in an operation of this nature would place the date of the origin of the venture some time before the 20th of April. As this was to be a combined naval and military endeavor, it is possible that planning, on a staff level, involving the Howe brothers, might well have been initiated as early as April 9 or 10.

COMPOSITION OF THE BRITISH REGULAR TROOPS

The part of the striking force composed of British regulars consisted of detachments of 250 men each from the 4th, 15th, 23rd, 27th, 44th, and 64th Regiments of foot. In addition, there were ten from the 17th Dragoons and a detachment of artillery to serve the six 3-pounders that were to accompany the expedition.[11] All these units were of experienced, regular British army regiments, each with a long and honorable tradition, and each having taken part in one or more battles in 1775-1776. The 4th, 23rd, and 64th had participated in the expedition to destroy the stores at Lexington,[12] and the 23rd, 44th, and 64th had participated in the raid on Peekskill one month prior (March 23, 1777).

BROWNE'S PROVINCIAL TROOPS

Separate mention must be made of the remaining body of troops that was to accompany Tryon and his 1,500 British regulars, 300 men from Governor Browne's corps called the Prince of Wales Loyal American Volunteers.[13] This was but one of several units being raised in and around New York City by such prominent Loyalists as John Peter DeLancy, John Bayard, and Montford Browne. The story of Loyalist participation in the war need not be treated here except to note briefly that thousands of Loyalists sought refuge within British lines, principally around their main bases of Boston (until evacuation), New York, and Charleston, and that "Thousands enlisted in provincial regiments officered by the Loyalists themselves and equipped like British regulars. These troops, acquiring discipline and experience, fought valiantly for their people and the empire. . . ."[14] In all, there were seventy-three Provincial Regiments or other units serving in the war.[15]

Montford Browne, the ex-Royal Governor of the Bahamas, had been capturd by the Americans earlier in the war but had been exchanged for Major General Stirling.[16] After his release, Browne appears to have devoted his time and energies to the raising of the aforementioned corps. This body of Loyalist troops was recruited and based at Flushing on Long Island, as evidenced by a recruiting advertisement that appeared in one of the Loyalist newspapers then being published at New York:

> The Royal and Hon. Brigade of the Prince of Wales Loyal Amer. Volunteers quartered at the famous and plentiful town of Flushing. Recruits taken also at Wm. Betts, sign of the Gen. Amherst, Jamaica. £5 bounty and 100 acres of land on the Mississippi, for three years, or during the rebellion. Present pay and free quarters. Clothing, arms, and accouterments supplied.[17]

Each of the provincial corps being raised appears to have drawn its strength from certain followings or geographic areas. Browne's corps seems to have been very popular with the Loyalists of Fairfield County, Connecticut. William Edgar Grumman, in his history, *The Revolutionary Soldiers of Redding, Connecticut*, documents the fact that numerous men from Redding served in this corps. Grumman is of the opinion that this recently-recruited corps was "largely, if not entirely, composed of Fairfield County Loyalists."[18]

At least two men from Danbury served with Browne on the raid, according to the interesting journal of Col. Stephen Jarvis—"In this [Danbury] expedition Munson Jarvis and William Jarvis were with the British and slept at my father's house the night they were in Danbury."[19] By way of explanation, Colonel Jarvis, as he himself explains in his journal, had been born and reared in Danbury but had left home prior to the raid due to a disagreement with his Loyalist father over his courtship of a young lady. Hearing erroneous tales that his father had been slain being circulated around New York after the raid, Stephen Jarvis approached the first officer ". . . that first fell in my way. It was with a Captain Lockwood, who piloted the British Army to Danbury."[20] Lambert Lockwood was raising a company as part of a provincial corps, called the Queen's Rangers, then forming at Kingsbridge. Young Jarvis subsequently joined this corps as a sergeant, rising to colonel by the end of hostilities. Like so many Loyalists, Jarvis moved to Canada after the war, and died in Toronto in 1840.

The inclusion of Browne's corps in the expedition would then seem most logical, as it contained men from most, if not all, the towns through which the British planned to operate. Tryon would have the advantage of the most detailed and intimate knowledge of terrain, roads, and the political sentiments of the population.

The histories of most towns concerned with the raid credit one of their local Tories with "leading the British to Danbury." It would seem most probable, however, that it was not one, but rather a succession of them serving with Browne.

All accounts of the expedition list Browne's corps as sailing from New York with the 1,500 Regulars; certainly this is the impression we receive from Robertson's entry of April 20-21 which enumerates the units that participated (including Browne's corps) and notes their embarkation in the North River.[21] H. M. S. Swan's log (one vessel that escorted the expedition) clearly indicates that Browne's corps of 300 Loyalists did not sail from New York with the contingent of British Regulars, but, rather, joined the force in Long Island Sound, en route from its embarkation point of Oyster Bay on Long Island.[22]

SIZE OF EXPEDITIONARY FORCE

There is some difference of opinion as to the size of the British force. Lacking Howe's orders to the regiments concerning the number of companies to be detached and the muster roll of each company, it is impossible to give a precise figure. Howe, however, in his letter to Lord Germain dated April 24, 1777, mentioned "a detached Corps of troops consisting of 1800 Rank and File. . . ."[23] This figure is supported by Captain Robertson in his diary entry for April 20:

Upon Information that the Rebels had collected a Great Magazine of Stores and Provisions at Danbury in Connecticut, a secret Expedition was set on Foot to Destroy it, consisting of 250 men from each of the Following Regts Vzt. the 4th, 15th, 23rd, 27th, 44th, 64th making 1500 men, also 300 Provincials of Governor Brown's Corps, a Detachment of Artillery, and 6 3-pounders and 10 17th Dragoons.[24]

It is clear that the figures given by those concerned must be considered rounded numbers or approximations, and not a precise headcount. Robertson's tally of 1,500 regulars, 300 provincials, approximately 35-40 artillery men needed to serve the six field pieces,[25] and 10 dragoons, gives us a total of nearly 1,850, which, while slightly higher than Howe's figure, is probably close to being correct. The 2,000 quoted by Hutchinson in his long report to Lord Percy[26] would appear to be incorrect, as would be a similar figure from the newspaper account of the raid by *The Connecticut Journal* dated Wednesday, April 30, 1777, which stated that

On Friday the 25th instant, twenty six sail of the enemy's ships appeared off Norwalk Islands, standing for Cedar Point, where they anchored at 4 o'clock P. M. and soon began landing troops; by 10 o'clock they had landed two brigades, consisting *of upwards of two thousand men* [italics mine]. . . .

This figure of 2,000 men, and, indeed, the entire account, quoted in part, from *The Connecticut Journal* of April 30, seems to have formed the basis for numerous accounts and histories. It is interesting to note, however, that the *Journal* account appears to have been copied almost word-for-word by the *New London Gazette* and published in their issue of May 9, 1777. It is this version that can be found in the many histories of Connecticut. The same article appeared again almost word-for-word in the *Pennsylvania Journal* of May 14, 1777.

The colonial figure must certainly have been an estimate, and Hutchinson's figure cannot be looked upon with any degree of credibility, as, unlike Captain Robertson, he was not associated with the expedition, but was merely a passenger aboard the packet *Mercury* proceeding down the Sound when it fell in with the little armada assembled off Compo Point. By his own words, he was "only about ten minutes on board *Senegal,* I could not possibly collect as many particulars as I wished."[27] This brief meeting took place on the 29th of April during the stress of re-embarking the force, as attested to in the log entry of that date of His Majesty's Sloop *Swan,*[28] surely not the proper circumstances under which an accurate report could be prepared.

Perhaps the officers commanding the expedition had no knowledge, themselves, of the precise figure. Possibly an 18th-Century British officer was not overly concerned with detailed statistics or the importance of enumerating private soldiers.

Robertson's report, from which we can approximate a figure of nearly 1,850, is basically supported by General Howe, and must stand as a reasonably accurate estimate of British strength employed in the Danbury raid. This figure would belie the more romantic versions to be found in some old histories where we see the British as a force of 2,500 men, or as William H. Burr in his often-quoted account states: "Tryon with his marching thousands."[29]

LACK OF HESSIAN PARTICIPATION

Despite some accounts, and local legend to the contrary, not one shred of evidence exists to support the contention that Hessian troops participated in the expedition. Participation by German mercenaries in this expedition would have been most unlikely in view of several circumstances. The stinging defeats to British arms in the closing weeks of 1776 had been made possible to a large degree by the failure of the Germans at Trenton under General Riall (one of several spellings) either to know about Washington's movements, or to repulse the American attack once it had begun. This blot on British arms could be wiped out only by British troops.

Secondly, if a political purpose were to be served by this expedition into Connecticut, the use of hired foreign troops could hardly be expected to serve that end.

Thirdly, the German troops in New York City were, as we have already seen, ill-prepared at this time to take the field, lacking, as they were, proper equipment.

Lastly, we learn from General Clinton that General Howe had no great enthusiasm for the employment of German troops, preferring Russians instead. Clinton reports that Howe told him the Germans "will not act with the same willingness as your northern friends [Russians], but we must make the best of them."[30]

NAVAL PARTICIPATION

The force thus described and enumerated, was to be transported by ships of the Royal Navy from New York City to its debarkation point on the coast of Connecticut. The naval participation is best described by Admiral Viscount Howe in his letter to Philip Stephens, Esquire, Secretary to the Lords Commissioners of the Admiralty:

Despatch No. 28 [H.M.S.]   Eagle [Flagship] off New York
April 23, 1777

... The General determining upon an attempt to destroy a very valuable magazine said to be formed by the rebels in the Province of Connecticut, several regiments were embarked in 12 transports [on] 21st instants to be landed on the coast of that Province, as Governor Tryon, who commands the troops, should require. I have committed the conduct of the naval department to Capt. Duncan of the Eagle. He is embarked in the Senegal and has the Swan also under his command, those sloops being deemed of sufficient force and most proper for the intended operation.[31]

From Admiral Howe's letter to Stephens, we also learn the names of the naval officers commanding the flat boats:

Dated May 18, 1777

. . . The service being critical and the navigation intricate, I committed the conduct of it to Capt. Duncan. The Capts. Malloy and Clayton commanding the flat boats under his orders. . . .[32]

USE OF A DIVERSION

As part of the strategy to be carried out with regard to the expedition to Danbury, an imaginative diversion was planned. We learn something of its composition and intent in Admiral Howe's letter to Stephens dated April 23, previously quoted in part:

. . . A diversion was thought fit to be made at the same time up the North River, 12 transports [the same number as the real striking force] in which a small corps of troops are embarked attended by Ambuscade, Mermaid, Daphne, Rose and Dependence Galley have been appointed for that service. . . .[33]

The small body of troops used in the diversion consisted of 150 men from the 57th Regiment and 150 provincials of Lieutenant Colonel Bayard's Corps.[34] Bayard's Corps was similar in nature and composition to that Montford Browne's.

A better diversion could not have been found. Howe undoubtedly knew that any move he might make that would appear to endanger American positions holding the key to the Hudson Highlands would divert attention from the force proceeding up Long Island Sound. The Hudson River-Peekskill area was still very sensitive following the small but successful raid on Peekskill carried out under the command of Colonel Bird one month prior to the Danbury expedition (March 23, 1777).[35] We shall meet Colonel Bird again, as he plays a role in the Danbury expedition. The diversion "up the North River" was to prove very successful, as we shall see as the story of the raid unfolds.

All was in readiness, then, for the expedition to proceed on its ambitious intent to destroy a rebel magazine. Like the earlier raid on Lexington, the British were operating from a base of sea power from which they marched into hostile territory. The force was, in numbers, approximate to that of Lexington. It was well-officered and consisted of well-equipped, disciplined, and battle-tested British regulars. Unlike the battle at Lexington, they enjoyed the element of surprise and a well-conceived diversion.

The Progress of
the Expedition to Danbury

THE FLEET LEAVES NEW YORK

All being in readiness, the force of approximately 1,550 British regulars crowded into ten of the twelve transports and set sail from their embarkation point in the North River at about 2:00 P.M. on Tuesday, April 22, 1777.[1] Since Browne's corps of 300 Provincials did not sail from New York with the main force of Regulars, it is probable that two of the twelve transports were empty. These were to be used to embark the Provincials at Oyster Bay. We can pick up these two transports by examining the *Halifax*'s log entry of April 22, 1777: "Fired a 4 pdr shotted and brought to the ———— and ———— transports bound to Oyster Bay: joined company."[2]

This can further be substantiated from a statement of regimental strength submitted to General Howe by Lieutenant Colonel Thomas Pattinson of the Prince of Wales Royal American Volunteers, dated April 21, 1777. In this report, the total strength of the above corps was given as 520 men, with 374 listed as present and fit for duty. Beside those listed as sick, on leave, etc., 37 are listed as "on command." This term was used to describe those men detached from the main body acting under orders. Lieutenant Colonel Pattinson reported: "1 Sargent and 21 Rank and File are On board the *Speedwell* and 1 Sargent and 14 Rank and File on board the Lady Standley."[3] The provincials, then, provided their own crews, and we learn the names of two of the twelve transports.

Traveling unescorted, the transports moved across the Upper Bay and into the East River. A glance at a map will quickly reveal that the East River is not actually a river, but, rather, an inland waterway or strait that connects New York Bay with Long Island Sound.

As they entered the East River, one of the transports ran onto a *chevaux-de-frise* opposite the Battery.[4] This underwater obstruction, made of heavy timbers and spiked with steel, was part of the defenses constructed by the Americans in 1776 in their attempt to deny the waterways to the British.[5] The transport "sprung off the *chevaux-de-frise* and got clear of other ships with good Management, or two if not three must have been drove [sic] on shore."[6] Narrowly averting a calamity, the transports proceeded up the East River without further incident.

The progress of the expedition by water can be traced through the ships' logs and muster books of the three armed vessels which escorted the transports.[7] Written with typical naval attention to detail, two of these vessels have already been identified as the sloop *Senegal*, Capt. Roger Curtis, RN, and the sloop *Swan*, Capt. James Ayscough, RN.[8] The third of the armed escorts was the brig *Halifax*, Lt. William Quarme, RN, commanding.

By Sunday, April 20th, the *Senegal* and *Swan* were moored off the Brothers, two small islands lying approximately N.W. of Rikers Island in the East River. The next few days were spent in normal shipboard routine and provisioning from several transports that arrived at the anchorage. In the *Senegal's* log entry of Wednesday, April 23, we are able to pick up the transports moving up the East River:

> 3 P.M. 12 transports and several sloops came through Hell Gate—at 4 P.M. unmoored, weighed and came to sail as did the Swan. At 6 [P.M.] anchored off City Island in 8 fathoms, Hart Island NE 1 mile. Fleet in company, Found her [H.M.S.] the Scorpion sloop. Came on board Governor Tryon, Sir. W. Erskine, Capt. Duncan and Lt. Watts.[9]

With the fleet at anchor off City Island, we might pause to note an interesting mystery. Where was General James Agnew, second in command of the expedition? Neither the log books nor muster books of the two sloops place him on board. *Senegal's* muster book enumerates a list of passengers attached to the expedition, but no mention is made of General Agnew:

> Maj. Gen. Tryon, Sir William Erskine, Major Holland, Capt. William Wynes, [Wemyss? Aide to Tryon] Lt. Beard, Capt Lockwood, entered and joined 22/4/1777 + servants.[10]

While we are left with the mystery of Agnew, the muster book entry quoted above does partially substantiate the statement of Colonel Jarvis to the effect that it was Lockwood "who piloted the British to Danbury." While not defining Lockwood's role, the muster book clearly establishes his presence with the expedition.

At 1:00 P.M., Thursday, April the 24th, *Senegal*, bearing the senior naval officer, Captain Duncan, made signal for weighing, and, with the transports following, proceeded up the Sound. Between the 4:00 P.M. and 5:00 P.M. log entries, another mishap occurred to one of the transports as she "got aground on the Stepping Stones."[11] These partially submerged shoals, still to be found on charts of the area, lie S.E. of City Island where they project into the main channel from Elm Point, Long Island, the present site of the Merchant Marine Academy.

The task of extricating the hapless transport from her predicament fell to the *Swan*.[12] With the assistance of her boats, the *Swan* managed to free the vessel at 8:00 P.M. but remained anchored off the Stepping Stones. At 5:00 A.M. on the morning of the 25th, the *Swan*, in company with four transports, made sail and rejoined the main body of the fleet at 9:00 A.M. anchored off Sandy Point, Long Island.[13]

Near this achorage is another danger to navigation. Romantically named, the Execution Rocks just out from Sands Point to a position near mid-Sound. After two near mishaps, Captain Duncan thought it prudent to take some precautions in regard to this menace to navigation. On Friday, April 25, he "placed a schooner by the Execution Rocks for the transports to avoid them."[14] From this point, Long Island Sound broadens with nothing to impede the progress of the fleet.

While still at anchor off Sands Point, the fleet was joined by the two transports bearing the 300 men of Browne's Provincial Corps.[15] The *Halifax* met the two transports proceeding alone and escorted them to Oyster Bay, where the Provincial troops were to be embarked. After assisting with the embarkation, *Halifax* parted company with the two transports, which proceeded on their own to rejoin the fleet.[16]

At 2:00 P.M., Thursday, April 24, the convoy weighed anchor, proceeded down the Sound, and came to anchor again at 6:00 P.M. with the Execution Rocks W. by S½ S. 2 miles. At 5:00 A.M., Friday, April 25, the convoy weighed anchor for the last time before arriving at the debarkation point. At 11:00 A.M., they were joined by the *Halifax* and by noon the convoy was complete and proceeding "about mid Sound."[17]

AMERICAN RESPONSES TO BRITISH PREPARATION

It might be well at this point to note American reactions to the activities and preparations necessary to form the expedition. The diversion "up the North River" had, incidentally, sailed at the same time as the main effort. Correspondence from Washington's headquarters at Morristown, New Jersey, clearly reflects the anxiety with which he awaited Howe's overdue spring offensive. Washington's meager force had to be in a position to meet one or more thrusts by the British, and, for this reason, any move or moves on the part of the British had to be interpreted correctly before the small American force could be committed to the field. As March moved into April, Washington was quite aware of the fact that Howe was beginning to bestir himself.[18]

Because it was nearly impossible to distinguish friend from foe, Tory from rebel, security, in the modern sense, was all but unknown. The diaries, letters, and journals of the period clearly indicate that movement of "civilians" was a relatively easy matter. The flurry of activity in the British camp caused by the expedition readying itself did not go unnoticed at Washington's headquarters.

Upon receipt of specific intelligence, Washington alerted General McDougall, holding the critical Peekskill area, to be aware of a possible move in his direction:

April 18, 1777   Morristown, N.J.
By three deserters who are just come in, we are informed that the 10, 37, 38, 52 Reg., laying upon Saten Island were ordered, the day before yesterday, April 16 to hold themselves in readiness to embark at an Hour's warning, the place of destination unknown.[19]

The units referred to by the deserters are not those that participated in the expedition. This would leave one to assume that the deserters had essentially the correct information but had incorrectly enumerated the units. Considering the time element and the fact that they were "to hold themselves in readiness to *embark*" would strongly suggest that they were part of the force readying itself for the expedition to Danbury.

Enclosed in a letter of April 23rd, Washington relayed further intelligence to General McDougall in the form of a letter that he (Washington) had received from Major General Adam Stephen.

April 22, 1777   New Ark, [Newark] N.J.
By a person to be depended upon, who left N.Y. yesterday, [April 21] A brigade consisting of the 15th, 17th, not exceeding 700 men, and he believes the 36th and 4th embarked the 20th at night and he suspects sailed up the North River yesterday morning to destroy Gen'l McDougall.[20]

In this letter, the regiments are correctly identified. Clearly, this must be the Danbury expedition being formed, but as late as the 23rd, Peekskill was still the suspected target. No mention of Danbury was made by Washington until April 25 in his letter to General Parsons:

April 25, 1777   Morristown, N.J.
I have this minute received some information, which seems to corroborate what the Tories have said, of the Enemy's designs against the Magazines at Danbury. I therefore desire you will order all the Men drafted in your State for this year, to be collected and inoculated there, that the circumstances and situation of the place will possibly admit, that they may protect the stores.[21]

Intelligence had correctly identified Danbury as the target, yet Washington's qualifying statement, "which seems to corroborate," indicates his uncertainty, and thus his unwillingness, to weaken the Hudson Highlands defense by moving McDougall's force from Peekskill to the defense of Danbury.

Washington's letter to General McDougall, dated the same day as his letter to General Parsons, does not indicate any undue alarm, nor does it even alert his commander at Peekskill to the same intelligence forwarded to General Parsons:

April 25, 1777 [the date of the landing at Compo]   Morristown, N.J.
As I have heard nothing further of the troops that embarked on the 20th, I can only recommend it to you to keep a vigilant look out for them.[22]

It is apparent from this correspondence that General Washington was well aware of the British activity in New York, and that there are positive indications that Danbury was to be the prime target. Howe's diversionary movements in the North River, and perhaps recollections of the March raid on Peekskill, prevented Washington from making more positive moves to protect the magazine of stores at Danbury. That the diversion was highly successful is best noted in Washington's letter to Gen. Clinton:

> 2 o'clock P.M. April 26, 1777:
> A letter from Gen' McDougall, this moment received, places their intentions beyond the power of misconception. Several transports have anchored at Dobb's Ferry, and mean, in my opinion, to divert our attention (if possible) from *their movements towards the Delaware*.[23]

Not only was the Commander-in-Chief aware of the probable threat to Danbury, but as early as *April 12th*, Governor Trumbull of Connecticut and the Council in Hartford were also apprised of the danger. As recorded in the minutes of Connecticut General Assembly,

> The Governor and Council on April 12, 1777 sent a letter to Gen. Silliman, [Commander of Militia] instructing him to keep the utmost vigilance over the enemy, who were supposed to be collecting in New York, in order to go up the North River, to destroy the Magazines at Danbury, and other places in that quarter, and to raise his brigade for defense, if he thought proper; to give the earliest intelligence to the Governor and Council, of every alarming appearance of danger in his department.[24]

In retrospect, it is difficult to understand why more positive steps to defend Danbury were not undertaken by Washington or Connecticut state officials. McDougall *would* commit his force after it was too late, and the militia would turn out, but again only after the outcome had been determined. Peekskill and the North River continued to be the points of greatest concern. Even on the 27th of April, when the British had begun their retreat from Danbury, the Connecticut General Assembly received a communication from Colonel Huntington at Danbury "that 18 ships with troops of the enemy, were going up the North River near Peekskill."[25] Possibly the Americans were of the opinion that Danbury was the diversion and the force moving up the North River was Howe's main effort. Suffice it to say, circumstances and British strategy were working to the advantage of the expedition as it neared its destination.

THE DEBARKATION

By noon of Friday, April 26, the fleet was nearing the landing area. Their orders "proposed that the debarkation should be made at Norwalk."[26] The Americans, however, had constructed coastal defense batteries at points along the shoreline of Fairfield County which necessitated a change of plans. At Fairfield (Groves Hill or Black Rock), there was a battery of considerable strength, six or eight guns, some of which were twelve and eighteen pounders. At Norwalk, the proposed landing site, there was a battery of six guns. The same was to be found at Stamford and Greenwich. At Stratford (Newfield or Bridgeport) harbor, at what is now Sea Side Park, there was a small fortified battery of two guns.[27] Even Darien was prepared to contest any hostile move. The *Halifax* ventured too near the Connecticut shore, and, as her log recorded, "the rebels came down and fired a swivel and several small arms at us—10 AM fired 4 x 4 pdr. shotted at the rebels on Long Neck [Darien]."[28]

All but one of the possible landing sites within reasonable marching distance of Danbury were protected by batteries. Only one place offered a safe anchorage and a gently-shelving and unprotected beach —the sheltered bay at the mouth of the Saugatuck River with the sandy beaches of Compo Point close at hand. It was here that the landing was to be effected.

Saturday, April 26, 1777,[29] from *Senegal's* log: ". . . At ½ past 5 P.M. anchored in four fathoms with a Spring in Satocket [sic] River, Cedar Point N NW ½ mile. . . ."[30]

The landing of the troops was in keeping with General Tryon's orders:

Senegal, April 23rd, 1777

Major Gen¹ Tryon's Orders.
   Capt. Wemyss of the 40th Reg¹ is appointed to Act as Adjut¹ Gen¹ to the Corps under his Command. The Troops to land in three divisions—The first, consisting of the 4th and 15th Reg¹˙ under the Command of Lieu¹ Col° Bird, who is to occupy the the most advantageous Ground to cover the landing.
   The 2ᵈ consisting of the 23ᵈ and the 27ᵗʰ Reg¹˙ under the Command of Lieu¹ Colo° Maxwell.
   The 3ᵈ consisting of the 44ᵗʰ and 64ᵗʰ Reg¹˙ under the Command of Major Hope.
   General Agnew will be pleased to disembark, any time after the 1st division has made good their landing, & give the other divisions such directions in regard to their forming as he may think necessary.
   Two Pieces of Artillery to be landed with the 1st division, & the Remainder to follow afterwards as soon as possible.
   As soon as the 1st Division had made good their landing, the Dragoons & Artillery to disembark. It is recommended to the Officers, to keep their Men, as silent as possible.
   The Troops to carry on Shore with them One Days Provision dressed, four days bread, a proportionable quantity of Salt (which the Men are to be carefull off,) and two days allowance of Rum,

which the Com^g Officers of Reg^{ts} will take care, to have mixed with Water.

So soon as the whole is landed, the Corps to form two Brigades. The 1st consisting of the 4th, 15th & 23^d Reg^{ts} to be Commanded by Genl Agnew. The 2^d consisting of the 27th 44th & 64th to be by Lieu^t Col° Maxwell.

As the Com^r in Chief was pleased in his Order of the 21st inst, expressly to forbid Plundering: It would make Genl Tryon very unhappy, should the Troops give him any occasion, to carry them into execution, which the nature & importance of the present Service will require him to do: He therefore places his full confidence that the Spirit of Honor which has so eminently distinguished the respective Corps now under his Comm^d will, with the known Attention of the Officers, sufficiently incite them to a strict obedience to the said Order.

No Boat is to be suffered to go on Shore, till the Troops land, without leave from Genl Tryon or Captⁿ Duncan.

All Horses that can be procured at landing, to be brought immediately to Genl Tryon.[31]

The debarkation began immediately upon anchoring. The 1st division, under Lieutenant Colonel Bird, landed at 5:00 P.M.[32] Once ashore, this force proceeded to secure the beachhead by occupying two commanding hills called Compo Hill and Bennets Rocks.[33] The remaining divisions landed in the order prescribed by Tryon, and by 11:00 P.M., the entire force was ashore and drawn up on Compo Hill.[34] The landing had been completely uncontested.

While the debarkation was taking place under the guns of the sloops *Senegal* and *Swan*, H.M.S. *Halifax* [Brig] sailed to Bridgeport, where she "saw a private brig lying in Black Rock Harbor."[35]

From 5 P.M. on Friday, April 26 until Monday, April 29 (7 A.M.), the *Halifax* was to remain on station at Black Rock, effectively blockading the American "privatier [sic]." The battery at Black Rock fired a total of thirteen shots at the *Halifax*, all falling short.[36]

It is difficult to estimate the amount of mischief this unknown American brig could have caused, had she been free to molest the British fleet lying at anchor at the mouth of the Saugatuck. H.M.S. *Halifax*, commanded by Lieutenant William Quarme, RN, must have felt that she was contributing to the success of the operation to have remained so long on station under fire from a shore battery.

AMERICAN REACTIONS TO THE LANDING

The Americans were, of course, well aware of the arrival of this force. In anticipation of just such a contigency, the selectmen of the various towns had appointed well-qualified individuals to keep watch. The most important of these lookout stations was located about six miles N.W. of what is now Bridgeport, atop Tashua Hill. This vantage point was the main intelligence center for the southwest portion of the state. Although there were other lookout sites, Tashua Hill provided the largest proportion of naval intelligence throughout the war.[37]

Local militia and units from Stamford and Norwalk assembled the night of the landing at Saugatuck, where they watched the movements of the enemy rather than foolishly attempt to oppose the landing.[38]

Messengers were sent to spread the alarm. General Gold Selleck Silliman began to assemble his militia,[39] and Generals David Wooster and Benedict Arnold at New Haven offered their services.[40]

Although British intentions could not be definitely ascertained at this point, it is clear that the Americans finally realized that Danbury was to be the ultimate objective. A rider was dispatched from Fairfield to Danbury bearing the news that a force of British, three to four thousand, had landed at Fairfield and were believed to be interested in the stores kept at Danbury. The rider arrived in Danbury at 3:00 A.M., Saturday morning.[41]

THE MARCH TO DANBURY

The British, drawn up in marching order, began their movement inland at 11:30 P.M., Friday, April 25.[42] As they proceeded up Compo Street (Road), they were fired upon by a small group of hastily-assembled militia under the command of Captain Disbrow.[43] These straggling shots caused some confusion among the Provincial troops at the head of the line of march, but only one officer and five or six men were wounded as a result of this brief encounter.[44] Those requiring medical attention (one officer and two men) were placed on an oxcart and returned to the ships. The officer, Captain Lymond, was kept aboard the *Senegal,* while the two men were placed aboard the hospital ship.[45]

Pressing on, Tryon's force proceeded along Compo Street until they came to Cross Highway, and then proceeded eastward. They continued down Cross Highway until they came to the road that leads from Fairfield to Redding, now Connecticut Route 58.[46] At a point some eight miles from the landing site, the British bivouacked for the few remaining hours of the night.[47]

The march inland on the road leading to Danbury dispelled whatever doubts remained concerning British intentions. A second messenger was dispatched to Danbury with this latest intelligence. His arrival about sunrise (Saturday, April 26) was the signal for the hasty evacuation of whatever public and private goods could be saved.[48]

Doctor Isaac Foster, an energetic and enterprising officer in charge of the medical suplies in Danbury, had prepared the more valuable stores in his charge for movement at the first alarm. With the arrival of the second messeenger, Dr. Foster personally supervised the removal of his medicines to the comparative safety of New Milford.[49]

Breaking camp on the morning of April 26, the British forces continued on their way towards Danbury. The only opposition they encountered was from the militia company of Redding under the command of Captain Read. Moving out to reconnoiter the enemy, this hastily-mustered company suddenly came upon the enemy at a place called Couche's Rock in what is now the town of Weston. In this unexpected encounter, several militiamen were captured; the remainder of the company fled back to Redding.[50] After passing through the naturally-defensive defiles at Gilbert Town and Jump Hill, at 11:00 A.M., the British arrived in Redding, where a halt was called for food and rest.[51]

Contrary to some lurid accounts of their brief stay in Redding, the British behaved well. There is no evidence to support the legend that the British troops wantonly destroyed the church. While the troops ate and rested, Generals Tryon, Agnew, and Erskine dined in the home of Squire Heron next to the Anglican Church. As the rector, the Reverend John Beach, was a Loyalist, there would have been no reason or justification to have destroyed the church.[52]

Squire William Heron deserves more than just a passing reference, for, in reality, this prominent citizen of Redding, Connecticut, was a double agent serving both American and British intelligence. Squire Heron's true role in the conflict was not brought to light until the papers of Sir Henry Clinton were made available to American historians in the 1880's. Should the reader care to learn more of the mysterious Squire Heron, he would do well to read the fascinating and thoroughly readable account of espionage during The Revolutionary War by John Bakeless, entitled *Turncoats, Traitors and Heroes.*[53]

No documentary evidence appears to exist that would link Heron to the raid on Danbury. But, in light of the good Squire's subsequent career, one cannot help but wonder what the topics of conversation were that day at lunch among three British generals, a Loyalist Anglican priest, and Squire William Heron.

Two prominent Patriots, Stephen Betts and James Rogers, as well as a young man, Jeremiah Sanford, were taken prisoner by the British in Redding. Tryon's force again took to the road on the last leg of its march to Danbury.[54] Robertson stated in his journal that the British stay in Redding lasted for an hour and a half, which would place the force on the road to Danbury at 12:30 P.M.[55]

Between Redding and Bethel, no opposition was encountered by the British troops, although several mounted men under arms were taken prisoner.[56] One of these prisoners might well have been Lambert Lockwood. Local accounts state that he had been sent to reconnoiter the approaching enemy, when, coming upon them suddenly, he was wounded and taken prisoner.[57]

After passing through Bethel without incident or pause, the British column deployed into a line as they prepared to enter Danbury.[58] Reference to a topographical map of the Danbury Quadrangle will reveal that the approach to Danbury from Bethel via Coal Pit Hill is basically a flat plain stretching from Thomas Mountain on the left to Shelter Rock on the right. Advancing in open order, with flanking units from the light horse extending to both high grounds, Tryon's force of 1,850 British regulars and Provincial troops advanced upon the all but undefended town.[59]

The time of the British entry is confirmed by Colonel Huntington's letter to General McDougall:

Danbury, 4 o'clock, P.M.   April 26, 1777

The enemy are just entered the town, and I am reduced to the hard necessity of leaving the plain and greatest part of the stores, and repairing to the heights with about 50 Continental Troops, and as many again militia. I had sent expresses every way for succours, but none has come worth mentioning. The enemy is said to be 2000.

I did not think it prudent to stay in this town to make any opposition, as the place is encompassed with heights and the number of the enemy to [sic] superior. I hope some continental troops from Massachusetts now at, or near, New Milford will be in here tomorrow.[60]

The British Occupation of Danbury

THE AMERICAN DEFENSE OF THE TOWN

American efforts to provide additional forces to protect the military stores at Danbury were belated and wholly ineffectual. On the 14th of April, General Samuel H. Parsons had ordered Colonel Chandler's regiment to rendezvous with other militia units at Danbury.[1] This was part of a plan to provide a measure of security for Danbury by ordering all newly-recruited men in Connecticut to be inoculated in that town. In his letter to General Washington, General Parsons stated:

Lyme [Connecticut] 15th April, 1777

I have Order[d]. all the Recruits lately Inlisted, who have not had the Smallpox, to Danbury where I shall Order those who are Detach[d]. in pursuance of the Inclos[d]. proclamation & resolve; as I suppose a Hospital open⁴. in that neighborhood, will be Suff⁴. to inoculate those who Chuse [sic] to Receive the Small Pox, & the Convalescents will be a Security to our Magazines of Provisions, which is at present unguarded.²

General Parsons' order, as did General Washington's to the same effect, came too late. Washington's letter to Parsons requesting that this be carried out was dated April 25, the date of the British debarkation at Compo.³

The Commander-in-Chief's reluctance to utilize General McDougall's force based at Peekskill some thirty-five miles away (in 1777)⁴ had placed the burden of defense squarely upon the shoulders of the meager forces then in Danbury.

This force, numbering about 150 men, was under the nominal command of Colonel Jedediah Huntington.⁵ The local militia company was commanded by Joseph P. Cooke.⁶ It is impossible to determine the exact numbers, but some histories have drawn upon the account given by the Reverend Doctor Thomas Robbins in his *Century Sermon*. Unfortunately, however, the good doctor was not an eyewitness to the events of the raid. The *Century Sermon* was written twenty-four years later, and Robbins undoubtedly drew upon the recollections and reminiscences of those then living in Danbury. With regard to numbers, Robbins merely stated that there was a small number of unarmed Continental troops in the town.⁷ Doctor Isaac Foster's account, written May 1, 1777, is contemporary to these events and somewhat richer in detail. He stated that a few Continentals were in transit to Peekskill, and that the militia had been mustered, but "their number was so inconsiderable I had no hope of the place being saved."⁸

In addition to Washington's strategic plan of draining Connecticut and Massachusetts forces to bolster the Hudson Highlands, there was still another reason for Danbury's defenseless condition. General Silliman's response to the landing on the 25th was an order that all militia be sent to him at Fairfield.

General Orders   Fairfield April 25
The enemy from 24 sail of shipping, have landed at Compo; their number is yet unknown, but it is of the last [?] importance to be ready to oppose them. You will therefore immediately muster your regiments, and march day and night, till you get here. As soon as you get 20 men of a company together send them on immediately under a proper officer, and send on the rest as fast as possible; bring all the ammunition you can get.

G. S. Silliman, Brig Gen
P.S.   There is a great want of ammunition. Flints are wanting. There are about one hundred Continental troops in this place double the number marched ye 24th on their way to Pekskill.⁹

Col. Huntington's response to General Silliman's orders is best seen in his letter to General McDougall:

Danbury   April 26th 1777   7 o'clock
Lieut Col. Sherman will march immediately for Peeks Kill with 40
or 50 men, being one half of all that are here at present. I hope about
100 men now on the road will be in here this night or tomorrow morning. The militia in this neighborhood are on the move toward Fairfield
in consequence of the express from General Silliman. I am sending an
express eastward to hasten troops and militia to this place and Peeks
Kill.

> and am Sir
> Your most ob'd—
> Jed Huntington[10]

Thus it can be seen that lack of a comprehensive defense, ill-conceived
disposition of troops, and confusion all contributed to the sad state of
defenses in Danbury.

Robbins tells us that the small number of troops "with the inhabitants generally withdrew from the town as the enemy approached."[11]
We learn from Doctor Foster, the medical officer, that every available
team and wagon had been utilized by the citizenry in their hurried
efforts to save their personal effects.[12] The lack of vehicles and military
manpower undoubtedly accounted for the failure of the Americans
to remove the bulk of the supplies to a point of safety.

The small force of Americans did not attempt a defense in any
sense, but, as Doctor Foster stated, retreated to high ground about the
town.[13] Here, from positions of comparative safety, they brought the
British troops under an unorganized fire. Captain Robertson, the British engineer officer, gives us the best, if not the only contemporary account:

> The Rebels Appeared about Danbury in a Body of 200 Scattered, they
> fired a few shots at a Distance. Wounded 3 of the 23rd [Regiment]
> while we were taking possession of the Rising Grounds about the Vil-
> lage.[14]

The disposition of the meager American forces can be substantiated by a letter from Colonel Huntington to General McDougall:

> Danbury   Hoits [Hoyt's] House   April 27th, 6 o'clock in the morning.
> I wrote you last Evening that the Enemy were in possession of the
> Town Plot and that the few Troops with me were then on the heights
> north of the Town where we still continue, small parties of Militia
> are coming in and 160 Cont¹. Massacuhsetts troops are near at hand
> from N. Milford intirely [sic] destitute of ammunition—those with me
> before had only two rounds—it is but small quantities that the Militia
> have with them no molestation can be given the Enemy without am-
> munition. There is a most advantageous Hill to plant a [Piece] or
> Two of artillery which would command the Town—General Silliman is
> between the Enemy and Fairfield with a large body of Militia.

> I am Sir
> Your Most hum Servᵀ
> Jed Huntington[15]

Having overcome this ineffectual show of resistance, the British forces moved to take full possession of the nearly deserted town. General Tryon quartered himself in the home of Nehemiah Dibble, located on South Street near Triangle Street. Generals Agnew and Erskine pressed on through the town via Town Street (Main Street) to secure the high ground north of the town, which, in 1777, centered about South Street.[16]

Documented details of the British occupation are sadly lacking. James Bailey's *History of Danbury* is rich in colorful anecdote and legend, but how much is fact is difficult to ascertain. A case in point is the alleged firing of cannon by the British in the vicinity of the present court house on Main Street. Bailey's account of the incident would have us believe that "the heavy balls, *six* and *twelve* pounders, flew screaming up the street, carrying terror to the hearts of the women and children, and dismay to the heads of the homes thus endangered."[17] As the British were armed with only *three pounders*, and the town was all but abandoned and undefended, Bailey's account is somewhat suspect. None of these cannonballs has ever been found.

THE EPISODE AT MAJOR STARR'S HOUSE

As the British moved up Main Street, an incident did occur that is supported by contemporary British and American accounts. An indeterminate number of "Rebels" began firing from the cover of a house upon the enemy troops drawn up in the street. This house, owned by Major Daniel Starr, stood on what is now the corner of Main and Boughton Street (site of the Danbury Police Department). Captain Robertson described the incident in these words: "When we entered the Street 7 Daring Rascals fired at us from a house that flank'd the street we were drawn up in. Two Companys of the 15th [Regiment] Attack'd them and put them to Death [,] Burning the house."[18] Bailey's account stated that there were three inside the building; Robbins' recollection was that four men were killed in the house.

This incident is further documented in the depositions taken before the January, 1778, session of the General Assembly. Ebenezer White testified that on the evening of April 26th, there were, in his house, a number of gentlemen (officers) belonging to the British army. One of these gentlemen, whom the deponent believed to be the Earl of Falkland's Son,[19] told him that there were several men, two of whom were Negroes, in the Starr house. The deponent added "that the said young gentlemen told him that one of the Negroes, after he had run him through, rose up and attempted to shoot him, and that he, the said Earl of Falkland's son, cut his head off himself."[20]

Two other depositions taken from Anna and Ebenezer Weed, who lived in the house "across the road opposite to Major Daniel Starr," essentially support that of Ebenezer White, but did not make any reference to the officer by name.[21]

Although the above deponent made reference to two Negroes, the weight of available evidence makes it clear that there was just one Negro involved in the shooting from the Starr house. Bailey's *History of Danbury* identified the Negro as a slave named Adams belonging to Samuel Smith of Redding who may have leased him to Captain Starr, which would account for the slave's presence in Danbury that fateful day.[22]

Bailey's account of the incident would seem to be partially incorrect, as evidenced by a petition to Hartford dated January 21, 1778, from Samuel Smith asking for damages resulting from the death of his slave identified in the petition simply as Ned:

> When the enemy of the United States of America made their incursion into the County to Danbury the sd Negro being a very zealous friend to the American cause turned out and went to Danbury to oppose the British troops and then and there bravely fought and opposed Sd troops till he was killed by the Enemy.[23]

Unless Samuel Smith was coloring his account to help his claim for compensation, we might consider that Ned was a volunteer who chose this cause of action of his own free will. Ned may well have been the first American to have died defending the stores at Danbury.

There is no supportive evidence to back up Ebenezer White's claim that Ned's execution had been carried out by the "Earl of Falkland's Son." Correspondence with the present (1974) Viscount Falkland indicates that the title is incorrect and that no member of his family served in the British army at that time. These facts are supported by *Burke's Peerage*. In short, it would seem as though the deponent simply did not identify Ned's assailant properly.

BRITISH PRACTICES WITH REGARD TO THE INCIDENTS ABOVE

We have then, sufficient evidence from both British and American sources to support this incident. The house and its inhabitants met the same fate as did others under similar circumstances in the retreat from Concord. As the alleged Earl of Falkland's son is reported to have said to Ebenezer White: ". . . it was our constant practice, where they found people shut up in a house and firing upon them, to kill them, and burn the house."[24] This is essentially the same practice as described by Lieutenant Barker of the 4th Regiment with regard to similar incidents that occurred on the retreat from Concord.[25] The diary of Lieutenant Frederick Mackenzie, Royal Welsh Fusiliers (23rd

Regiment), adds further weight to the argument that those men who were slain in Major Starr's house were not singled out for special acts of barbarism, but were killed according to the practice of the day. Lieutenant MacKenzie tells us that in the retreat from Concord "the Soldiers were so enraged at suffering from an unseen Enemy that they forced open many of the houses from which the fire proceeded, and put to death all those found in them."[26]

PREPARATION FOR THE DESTRUCTION OF THE STORES

The incident at Major Starr's house marked the last flurry of resistance; Danbury was now fully secured by British forces. Generals Agnew and Erskine established their quarters in the house of Benjamin Knapp which stood on the N.E. corner of what is now the corner of Main and White Streets.[27] This area was then on the outskirts of the town but close to the ring of pickets established on high points of ground to protect the approaches to the town.[28] All that remained was to collect the military stores. This the British immediately began to do, although Captain Robertson reported that the troops were "very much fatigued."[29]

BRITISH ATTEMPTS TO REMOVE STORES

The evidence is clear that the British had intended to carry away all of the stores that circumstances would permit. General Howe's letter to Lord Germain, dated New York, 22 May 1777, stated:

> General Tryon having intelligence that the whole force of the country was collecting to take every advantage of the strong ground he was to pass on his return to the shipping and *finding it impossible to secure carriages to bring off any part of the stores, they were effectually destroyed.*[30]

Had circumstances been favorable, Tryon would have been able to secure large quantities of food and other materials for the British forces in New York. As we have already seen, shortages of all kinds were a pressing problem for General Howe. Also, we learn from the journal of Ensign Thomas Glyn (attached to Howe's headquarters in New York) that tents were in short supply at New York. He stated in his entry of May 9, 1777, that "the Commanding Officers of corps will give orders for immediately repairing at as little expence as possible the Tents they have in store that are fit."[31] Had General Tryon been able to carry off the tents alone, it would have been a stroke of good fortune for General Howe who was faced with the prospect of opening the spring campaign with insufficient camp equipage.

Tryon's decision to destroy the stores was influenced to an equal degree by the gathering of substantial American forces at Bethel. General Silliman, residing in Fairfield, Connecticut, upon receipt of the alarm, began to muster the militia units under his command and then proceeded to follow the British line of march. He arrived in Redding Ridge at 8:00 P.M. on the 26th of April.[32] Major General David Wooster and Brigadier General Benedict Arnold arrived in Redding shortly thereafter, riding from New Haven with what forces could be collected.[33]

It is important to note that Benedict Arnold, who was to play such a large role in these and later events, was home on leave, in New Haven. He was staying at the home of his sister while sulking over real and imagined slights, notably, the promotion by Congress of officers junior to himself, despite his heroic contributions to the American cause. It is quite possible that Arnold would have resigned his commission but for the events that were to take place in the next few days.[34]

With General Wooster assuming command of those forces that had assembled at Redding, the Americans marched to Bethel in a driving rain, arriving at 11:30 P.M. There they bivouacked for the night, determined to contest Tryon's return march.

The time of their arrival in Bethel, and the size and the condition of the militia can be read in General Arnold's own words:

Arnold to McDougall
W. Red'ing
Ap'. 27th, 1777
10 o'clock P.M.

Last night at half past Eleven, Gen'. Wooster, Gen'. Silliman and myself with Six Hundred Militia arrived at Bethel, eight miles from Danbury. The Eccessive Heavy rains render'd their Arms useless, and many of the Troops were much fatigued having march'd thirty Miles in the Course of the day without Refreshment.[35]

SIZE AND SCOPE OF MILITIA FORCE

With regard to the size of the militia force, we are again hampered by a lack of contemporary estimates. Most accounts place the number of militia assembled at Bethel at about 500.[36] There is an indication from Kemble's journal that British estimates placed the figure much higher. Kemble reported the American force at Bethel as "a Body of near fifteen hundred men."[37] This grossly-exaggerated picture of American strength was to cause General Tryon some concern.

While specific numbers are uncertain, the records give a clear picture of the extent of the alarm and the response to it. Hinman's

Historical Collection notes that many towns from a remarkably wide radius of Danbury sent their militia to repel the British troops. Towns as distant as Goshen, Connecticut, reported sending fifteen men or more to Danbury.[38] Litchfield sent the last fourteen men fit for active service.[39] Numerous claims for compensation, as submitted to the General Assembly, are also helpful in revealing the towns that participated. To the east of Danbury, the alarm reached at least as far as Wallingford, as witnessed by the claim of one Aaron Ives of that town for baggage and horse lost at Compo Hill.[40]

While it is relatively easy to document the participation of militia from a wide area that would include New York State, it is difficult, if not impossible, to determine the numbers present at any particular point. As these militia units, ranging in size from whole companies to small parties, joined the running battle that ensued, their numbers swelled, but any figure given must be considered an estimate.

THE DESTRUCTION OF THE MAGAZINES

Realizing that there was no possibility of removing the stores, the order was given to destroy them. Most of the stores were kept in the unfinished Anglican Church, then located on South Street. The historian Benson J. Lossing, who visited Danbury to speak to the three survivors of April, 1777, tells that the church was filled to the galleries with the stores.[41] Out of deference to the Church of England, however, the stores were removed to the borders of the street and burned.[42] Stores kept in a barn belonging to Nehemiah Dibble were taken out and added to the fire, the barn being spared, as Dibble was a Tory and General Tryon's host. Another nearby barn, filled with grain, was burned with its contents.[43]

THE CONDUCT OF THE BRITISH TROOPS

Bailey's *History of Danbury* and numerous other accounts, paint a sordid picture of events that night. Hollister, from whom accounts appear to stem, tells of the drunken disorderliness of the enemy. His description would leave us to believe that Danbury had been visited by Attila the Hun, rather than by General Tryon.

Purportedly given to him by a revolutionary soldier, Hollister provides us with a sample of the prose that has colored many later narratives:

> Hundreds lay scattered at random, where ever the palsying demon had overtaken them; some in the streets with their faces blackened with smoke and soiled with earth; others sprawling in the dooryards, and others still, with wild excitement, holding themselves up by fences and trees, or grasping fast hold of each other, called loudly with oaths and curses to be led against the rebels.[44]

As the town was completely occupied by British troops (drunk or sober), it would not be plausible to imagine this "Revolutionary soldier" walking about observing the proceedings. Clearly, he was not eyewitness to those events, and Hollister's description cannot be taken without at least several proverbial grains of salt. Veteran soldiers will do many things when drunk, but begging to be led against the enemy is hardly one of them.

In the complete absence of any first-hand account, we are left to draw our own conclusions as to what transpired in Danbury on the evening of April 26th and the early hours of April 27th. As sizeable quantities of rum, brandy, and wine were destroyed, and soldiers being what they are, it is quite probable that isolated instances as described above did occur. But to suggest, as many accounts do, that the entire force of 1,500 British regulars and 300 Provincial troops were totally incapacitated by reason of drink,[45] is to ignore the training and discipline of these men under professional commissioned and non-commissioned officers. The conduct and discipline of the British soldier on this raid, and in other actions of the war, would not lead one to believe that six regiments, described by Howe's secretary as "the Flower of the Army," would cease to function as a military organization in the face of a few barrels of rum.[46] The Orderly Book kept by Captain Knight dated May 2, 1777, would indicate to us that the Commander-in-Chief thought well of the conduct and discipline of the men on the expedition. After extending thanks to General Tryon and the officers, Howe stated that "the Regularity of the Men, reflects credit upon the Discipline of the Army and does them great honor."[47]

THE DESTRUCTION OF PRIVATE PROPERTY

Tradition tells us that the work of destruction in Danbury was carried out in two distinct stages. The first stage (late Saturday, April 26) was limited to the military stores themselves and the several private structures housing them. The second stage is purported to have begun after General Tryon was informed by Tories of the American forces gathering in Bethel, some two miles away. This last stage is alleged to have been carried out for purely vindictive reasons. We are told that in the early hours of Sunday morning, the buildings owned by Tories were marked with a cross drawn with a piece of lime. These buildings were to be spared, while the torch was to be set to the rest.[48] Unfortunately for local legend, this cannot be supported by any contemporary account. Again, we are at a loss to give an accurate timetable or description of the events that took place in the early hours of April 27, 1777. Lacking credible documentation, the best that can be ascertained is that "about twenty dwelling houses, with a number of barns, stores, and other buildings, were destroyed."[49] This estimate of damage was determined by a committee appointed by the General Assembly in May of 1777 upon a memorial of the selectmen of Danbury. The committee arrived in Danbury on June 3, 1777, when it began to take sworn testimony from those suffering damage. Based upon the sworn depositions and "other evidence," the committee fixed the damage at £16,181.1.4. The findings were accepted by the Assembly and ordered to be lodged on file for future compensation.[50]

An objective examination of the few facts available to us would seem to belie the lurid tales of wanton destruction. The population of Danbury in 1777 was approximately 2,500 (based upon the census figure of 2,470 in 1774).[51] If we estimate the number of persons per dwelling at six, we arrive at a further estimate of four hundred dwelling units in Danbury at the time of the raid. In addition to the estimated number of dwelling units, there certainly must have been an equal number of barns, stores, shops, taverns, etc. If we compare the known number of dwellings destroyed (twenty), with the estimated number of such dwelling units in Danbury at that time (four hundred), we are left with three possible explanations for the relatively small amount of damage done.

The least plausible explanation is that approximately three hundred and eighty homes were marked with white crosses identifying them as belonging to Tories and thus friendly to the Crown. William Hanford Burr tells us that "firebrands had been applied to every home in the village, *except those of the Tories.*"[52] There is no evidence to support this ludicrous notion. Danbury's response to the raid, and to the war in general, clearly indicates that the majority of its citizens, like those of the State of Connecticut, were "ever inimical to the British Interests."[53]

The second theory would have us believe that the British were interrupted in their efforts to burn the town by the growing menace of the American militia. Supposedly, twenty homes were all that could be fired as the British hurriedly evacuated the town. With the British arrival in Danbury at 4:00 P.M. on the 26th, and their departure on the 27th at 8:00 A.M.,[54] we can compute the British to have had complete and uncontested control of the town for sixteen hours. Surely they had ample time to have completely destroyed Danbury, if this had been their intent.

Only the last explanation is reasonable in the light of the circumstances. An indeterminate number of structures housed the stores and, in British eyes, were legitimate military targets. These were destroyed with the stores by fire. An equally indeterminate number of structures probably caught fire accidently. Lastly, it is not inconceivable to suspect that some were fired for vindicative or retaliative reasons and, perhaps, for sheer vandalism.

If we accept the theory that one of the reasons for the raid on Danbury was political, then it is inconceivable that General Tryon hoped to win that political victory in Connecticut by wanton acts of destruction of private property. In none of the British documents relating to the raid is there so much as a hint that the expedition was undertaken for punitive reasons.

General Tryon, in repeating Howe's order of April 21, clearly set forth the attitude of the expedition with regard to its expected conduct. In his letter of April 23 (documented and quoted in full in Chapter III), General Tryon stated that

> as the Com' in Chief was pleased in his order of the 21'' inst. *expressly to forbid Plundering;* It would make Gen' Tryon very unhappy, should the Troops give him any occasion, to carry them into *execution,* which the *nature & importance of the present Service* will require him to do: He therefore places his full confidence that the Spirit of Honor which has so eminently distinguished the respective Corps now under his Comm⁴ will, *with the known Attention of the Officers, sufficiently incite them to a strict obedience to the said Order.*[55]

While the admonishment is expressly concerned with plundering, it is difficult to imagine that the troops were forbidden to plunder while being given license to comit arson against private property.

The available evidence is insufficient to provide a sweeping indictment of British conduct while in Danbury. There is, however, evidence that would intimate that some Americans took the opportunity to plunder and engage in acts of arson in the confusion immediately following the British evacuation of the town. Shortly after the raid, representations were made to the General Asembly of Connecticut by those citizens of Danbury who had suffered losses. In a "most pathetic memorial," they charged "that our own people of the militia, and others raised among us of the continental army should be so abandoned to all the feelings of humanity as to rob and plunder the remains of what the enemy have left to the poor and distressed inhabitants; and some have been even so daring as *after the enemy are gone off to set fire to houses and buildings,* under the pretence of their belonging to some inimical inhabitants of this state."[56]

As a result of this indictment, Governor Trumbull, in pursuance of a resolution by the General Assembly, issued a lengthy proclamation (May, 1777) that was couched in the strongest of language. In effect, it demanded that all guilty parties return to legal authority all goods, etc. plundered at Danbury. Should this be done, they "shall be discharged from all and every prosecution and penalty."[57]

Failure to heed the proclamation would make those guilty fully liable, under the state laws for theft and larceny, to prosecution. Further, Governor Trumbull ordered that the authorities, from each of the towns sending militia to the alarm, investigate those individuals to ascertain the guilty. Should Continental troops be involved, the company and battalion should be noted. This information would be turned over to the Governor who, in turn, would submit it to some general officer "That justice may be done."[58]

The melodramatic accounts of "the Burning of Danbury" are not supported by any objective analysis of the available facts. The damage to private property, from whatever cause, was relatively slight in proportion to the size of the town. This was war. The military stores were a legitimate target, as were the structures that housed them. It makes no difference whether the buildings were offered freely by their owners, or whether they had been commandeered by state or local authorities to house the stores; they *were* the magazine and, as such, were military targets.

We may never know, with certainty, the circumstances surrounding the destruction of the non-military structures. From the details related above, it would seem reasonable to suspect that some caught fire from the burning stores. This is what General Howe intimated in his communication to Lord Germain, No. 54, New York, 22 May, 1777: ". . . in the execution of which the village was unfortunately burnt."[59]

In quoting from the communication above (No. 54 Howe to Germain), Bailey writes: "On the 27th, in the morning, the troops *gutted* Danbury. . . ."[60] This is incorrect; the italicized word should be read as "quitted."[61] This was undoubtedly an honest mistake on Bailey's part, but, unfortunately, it leaves the reader with the wholly incorrect assumption that the firing of the town had been deliberate.

Some buildings were, perhaps, fired for punitive or vindictive reasons. Should this be true, it would seem that the Tories of Browne's Corps would be more suspect than would the British Regular who, in all likelihood, fought with little sense of personal involvement.

Lastly, Governor Trumbull's proclamation must be taken as sufficient evidence to place a portion of the blame for looting and arson on the shoulders of some Americans. It is impossible to state just how many structures can be rightfully charged to any one of the probable causes.

As the only recorded deaths in Danbury were the indeterminate number (3-7) slain in Major Starr's house, we cannot subscribe to the tales of slaughter alluded to but not substantiated through documentation, in the old histories. Those brave men who so foolishly chose to harass the British were dealt with in the prescribed manner of the day.

In their primary objective of destroying the rebel magazine, the British were eminently successful. Most accounts of the stores destroyed are taken from an enclosure to Sir William Howe's dispatch No. 54 to Lord Germain dated May 22, 1777. Following is his list of stores destroyed in Danbury:

> *Return of the Stores, Ordnance, Provisions etc. as*
> *nearly as could be ascertained found at the Rebel's*
> *Stores and destroyed by the King's troops at Dan-*
> *bury in Connecticut April 27, 1777.*
>
> A quantity of ordnance stores with iron, etc.; 4,000
> barrels of beef and pork; 1,000 barrels of flour.
> 100 large tierces of biscuit: 89 barrels of rice:
> 120 puncheons of rum: Several large stores of wheat,
> oats and Indian corn in bulk, the quantity there-
> fore could not be ascertained. 30 pipes of wine;
> 100 hogsheads of sugar. 50 hogsheads of molasses:
> 20 casks of coffee; 15 large casks filled with medi-
> cines of all kinds. 10 barrels of salt petre.
> 1020 tents and marquees
> A number of iron boilers
> A large quantity of hospital bedding, etc.
> Engineer, pioneer and carpenters' tools
> A printing press complete.
> Tar, tallow, etc.
> 5,000 pairs of shoes and stockings.[62]

Howe's list of materials destroyed appears to have been based upon one prepared by Captain Robertson. As the engineering officer of the expedition, it was within his province to supervise the destruction of the magazine. Robertson's list, then, is of considerable interest, in that it enables us to check the validity of Howe's report to Lord Germain.

Return of the Stores destroyed at Danbury nearly—
Between 3 & 4000 Barrels of Pork and Beef—
1000 Do   Flour
80 Hogsheads Biscuit
10 Barrels   Saltpetre
100 Do   Rice
60 Hogsheads Rum & Brandy
20 Do   Different Wines
10 Casks Medicines
upwards of 1000 Tents and some Marquis
60 Iron Kettles
A Quantity of Hospital Bedding and Sheeting
Some new Waggons [sic] and Intrenching tools

```
  400  Axes helved with handles
    5  Barrels of Nails
    2  Barrels of Printing Types
    2  Do      Stock Locks
  100  Do      Sugar Molasses and Coffee
   20  Do      Tar
 5000  Pairs Shoes and Stockens [sic]
```
Some ordnance Stores and a quantity of other Articles
for the use of the Army, the Quantity of which could
not be ascertained, such as Wheat, Indian Corn, Oats,
etc. A Quantity of Iron that could not be Destroy'd.[63]

A careful comparison of the two lists will reveal that the technique
of preparing communiques by the military for "home consumption"
is very old. In almost every category of stores destroyed, Howe's figure
exceeds that of Robertson. Two barrels of printing types become a
printing press complete. A *total* of 100 barrels of sugar, molasses, and
coffee become 100 hogsheads of sugar, 50 hogsheads of molasses, and
20 casks of coffee. Ten casks of medicine are reported to London as
"15 large casks filled with medicines of all kinds." Howe, like all commanders, evidently wanted to present his achievements in the best
possible light. A glowing report of success would help to placate the
critics of his inaction. But even by Robertson's more conservative
estimates, the material destroyed was a serious blow to the American
cause, plagued, as it was, by continued shortages of all kinds.

FACTORS INFLUENCING THE SUDDEN RETREAT FROM DANBURY

Having achieved his purpose at the cost of a few wounded, General Tryon decided it would be wise to commence his retreat to the
safety of the shipping. He was aware of the growing numbers of
Americans at Bethel who were preparing to contest his retreat, should
he attempt to return by the same route. To be sure, the British had
grossly exaggerated American strength at Bethel, and this, plus Tryon's
determination to "avoid Mr. Arnold," decided the issues.[64] The retreat
would be made by a different route.

General Tryon had good cause to respect Benedict Arnold. The
energy and skill of Arnold were well known to the British. Referring
to General Arnold in his journal, Glyn noted that

> he gave a great specimen during this War that tho ignorant of a Mili-
> tary Education & of all Military Science, yet by great resolution and
> a mind full of enterprise, he became a most excellent Partisan and
> skillful in the management of Light Troops.[65]

This generous estimate of Arnold's abilities rested upon his exploits
in the first two years of the war.[66] The British were well aware of his

role in the capture of Fort Ticonderoga, his march from Cambridge to Quebec through the wilderness in the middle of winter, his energy in building a fleet of ships on Lake Champlain, and his subsequent delaying action at Valcour Island.

The decision was made to avoid the American forces at Bethel by making a wide sweep through Ridgebury, Ridgefield, and Wilton, and thence to the ships lying at anchor off the beach at Compo. Marching up what is now Wooster Street, past the cemetery that was to be the first resting place of General Wooster, the British troops "quitted Danbury." The time was "about 8 o'clock," Sunday, April 27, 1777.[67]

Robertson's time of departure can be supported by a letter to General McDougall from one John Feild (or Field?). In addition, we can see that even by noon of the 27th, the intentions of the British were still not clear to the Americans:

To Gen'l. McDougal [sic]
at Peeks kill   Sunday 12 o'clock April 27, 1777
The Enemy left danbury [sic] at about eight o'clock this Morning, and now are at Ridgbury [sic]. It is uncertain what Road they will take, whether the Peekskill or Ridgefield, we shall be able to inform you if they continue their march in about an hour, When known shall send by express.

> Yr. hble. Serv't
> John Feild

Their force is suposed to be from 1500 to 2000.[68]

48

THE AMERICAN RESPONSE TO THE BRITISH RETREAT

General Tryon's decision to reach the safety of the shipping via Ridgefield presented a new problem for the American forces at Bethel. If the British were not going to force the passage through Bethel and return the way they came, what was their ultimate objective?

In General Arnold's correspondence to General McDougall, we learn not only of the disposition of American troops around Bethel, but also of the suspected intentions of the British based upon the initial direction of their march.

Wt. Red'ing   [Connecticut]   Ap¹ 27ᵗʰ, 1777
                                                         10 o'clock P.M.

> . . . At 6 this Morning we divided the Troops into two Divisions, being uncertain if they would return Via fairfield [sic] or Norwalk one division was station'd on each road, on a cross road where they could support each other—we have this minute In-formation that at 9 this Morning the Enemy set Fire to the Meeting House and most of the Buildings in Town, and had taken the Rout [sic] to Newbury [Ridgebury], leading either to Peeks Kill or Tarry Town. We imagine they are destin'd for the latter as we hear they landed Eight Hundred Men there Yesterday morning we propose following them immediately in hopes of coming up with their Rear. I hope you will be able to take them in front. Our Loss at Danbury is great but I hope not 'irreperably [sic]. I am with esteem
>
>   Sir
>   Yʳ mo Obedᵀ & ᵇᵇˡᵉ ˢᵛᵗ·
>   B. Arnold¹

The British were still deriving considerable strategic effect from their diversion up the North River. In the minds of the three American generals, two possibilities had to be considered as a result of the movement of the British due west. One possibility was that the enemy intended to reembark in the North River rather than at Compo. The second contingency which had to be considered was that Tryon's ultimate objective, after destroying the stores at Danbury, was to attack Peekskill as part of a concerted effort up the North River.

There is no evidence to support the contention that either of these two suppositions had been planned by General Howe. Robertson noted in his journal that the British intended to "return to the Ships by the way of Ridgefield."²

Generals Wooster, Arnold, and Silliman decided that one division would harass the British rear, while the other would attempt to block or retard the British progress through Ridgefield. General Wooster assumed command of the smaller force that would attack the rear, while Generals Arnold and Silliman began a forced march to Ridge-field with the larger one. Estimates of American strength again vary widely. Wooster probably had between 200 to 300 men, while Arnold, commanding the larger force, probably had between 400 to 500. Robertson placed the figures somewhat higher, estimating Arnold's force at 700 and Wooster's at 400.[3]

Upon receipt of Arnold's letter apprising him of the situation, General McDougall decided to take independent action. His letter to General Clinton, his subordinate at Fort Montgomery,[4] gives us his intentions and also his continued concern for the safety of Peekskill:

27 April 1777

Dear Sir

Time will only permit me to inform you, that the Enemy have left Danbury, and I have some prospect of doing something with the Enemy, by a forced march to Bedford. N.Y. There are a full Company of Militia at Fort Independence; and about Two Comp.s of Militia & Guards on Baggage, you will do the best you can with ships and Colo. Willetts at Fort Constitution, till I Return, which will be whenever I loose [sic] all prospects of Overtaking the Enemy, or the Northerly wind (Keaps), Open any letters to me from Gen'l Washington, and give the best answer you can.[5]

Based upon the information received from General Arnold, General McDougall's move to Bedford was excellent stategy. A glance at the map will reveal that Bedford lies directly on a line drawn between Ridgefield and the Tarrytown-Dobbs Ferry area. Had General Tryon planned to reach the North River, the final history of the British expedition into Connecticut might well have been one of utter disaster. General McDougall's force of 1,200 men and one field piece at Bedford,[6] and Wooster and Arnold's forces of nearly equal size bringing up the rear, would have been in an excellent position to jeopardize the success of the British withdrawal.

As the British retreated slowly down the road leading to Ridge-bury, encumbered by "five ox teams, fifty or sixty cattle and the same number of sheep," the Americans were moving cross-country to intercept them at Ridgefield.[7] The exact route taken by Generals Wooster and Arnold is unknown. Route 7, through Sugar Hollow, which is to-day the main road from Danbury to Ridgefield, was, at that time, non-existent. Reference to a map of the region will indicate that the American forces moving from Bethel to Ridgefield had to intersect the Sugar Hollow ravine at some point, and then follow the course of what is now Route 7 to Ridgefield. There is nothing in the contemporary accounts to suggest that the American forces at Bethel passed through Danbury on the heels of the British who turned west on the road to

Ridgebury (Miry Brook Road) while the Americans pressed south-ward through the wilderness of Sugar Hollow. It is more likely that Wooster and Arnold moved directly from Bethel through West Red-ding over existing roads to the Salt Pond (Lake Waubeeka) area. The remaining distance through the wilderness to existing roads in Ridge-field would have been relatively easy for a determined and enterprising man like Benedict Arnold who had marched through the wilderness from Massachusetts to Quebec.

ROUTE OF THE BRITISH RETREAT

The British, unaware of the American endeavor to intercept them at Ridgefield, marched down the road to Ridgebury. The route they took carried them down the Miry Brook Road, named, as legend would have it, because some enterprising Americans destroyed a bridge over the brook (Wolf Pond Run) causing some of the British artillery pieces to become mired. Valuable time was lost by General Tryon, as a temporary bridge of rails had to be constructed to enable the heavy equipment to pass.[8]

The only reference to this delaying tactic that has come to light is in a letter from McDougall to Washington apprising the Command-er-in-Chief of the events at Danbury: "Peekskill, 27 April 1777 . . . I have not been able to learn that one musket has been discharged against the Enemy or any other opposition given than the taking up [of] one bridge."[9] McDougall, of course, was not an eye-witness to the alleged destruction of the bridge but was merely passing on in-formation he had received. It seems unlikely that the loss of a bridge over a brook this small would have been anything more than a minor inconvenience, if, indeed, the incident did take place.

From the Miry Brook Road, the British troops marched over what is now called the George Washington Highway to Ridgefield. Here they wheeled south, passing through the village without incident. This southerly course (down the George Washington Highway) placed the British line of march parallel to the probable line of march of the Americans hurrying through Sugar Hollow some two miles to the East.

At a point where the George Washington Highway joins the North Salem Road (Route 33), the British set fire to the grist mill of Isaac Keeler.[10] The mill stood at the northern end of Lake Mamanasco near the junction of the two roads. Destroyed with the mill was a quantity of ground grain, described by General Howe in his report as "100 barrels of flour and a quantity of Indian Corn."[11] Robertson, again, gives us a more conservative estimate of "50 Barrels of Flour and a Quantity Indian Corn."[12]

Still unaware of American efforts to intercept them, the British force continued their march southward down the North Salem Road leading to Ridgefield. The rear of their column was now about two miles from the village of Ridgefield, at a point where Barlow Mountain Road joins the North Salem Road. It was at or near this point that the first of three engagements took place. Collectively, these three encounters are known as "The Battle of Ridgefield."

THE FIRST ENGAGEMENT

General Wooster, with his force of militia, advanced over Barlow Mountain Road where he fell upon the rear of the unsuspecting British column still enjoying their halt for rest and food. The encounter was very brief, but its suddenness enabled the Americans to capture a number of the enemy and make them prisoners. The old accounts usually credit Wooster with taking forty prisoners, but, in the light of available evidence, this figure would seem too high. In General Howe's return of the *Killed, Wounded and Missing*, the total number missing is given at twenty-seven.[13] As this figure would include any men taken by the Americans, we must conclude that forty is too generous a figure. The *Connecticut Journal* of May 7, 1777, stated that

> Last Friday 15 prisoners taken at Danbury were brought to this town [Hartford] and delivered to the care of the Committee.[14]

As there were no British prisoners taken at Danbury, the *Journal* reference is obviously to those taken by Wooster in his initial assault. The more conservative figure of fifteen prisoners taken is further supported in a letter from Huntington to McDougall, April 28: ". . . I find we have killed of the enemy in all yesterday's skirmishes twelve-thirteen prisoners including some wounded."[15]

THE SECOND ENGAGEMENT

General Tryon, now realizing that his retreat was not to proceed unimpeded, continued his march to Ridgefield. Meanwhile, General Wooster continued his harassment of the British rear. At a point one mile south of the first engagement, the pressure and audacity of Wooster's tactics caused the British to believe an assault in force was imminent. As legend has it, Wooster saw an opportunity to capture one of the field pieces with which the British rear guard was equipped. The rear guard faced about and fired upon the Americans, one ball bringing down General Wooster's horse. Mounting a horse belonging to one of his aides, the dauntless Wooster was attempting to rally his raw militia troops with a cry of "Come on, my boys, never mind such random shots! Follow me!" when a second ball struck him in the groin knocking him from the horse.[16]

The loss of General Wooster so dispirited the Americans that they broke off the action. Command of the forces harassing the British rear fell to Captain Stephen Rowe Bradley who reorganized the militia and then pressed on to join the main American force under Arnold.[17]

GENERAL WOOSTER'S DEATH

The ball that struck General Wooster coursed upward, apparently damaging his spinal cord and, as the old accounts tell us, he was left paralyzed. ˙ s wound was dressed by a Doctor Turner and he was carried back to Danbury by carriage.[18]

Ironically, the mortally-wounded Wooster was placed in the home of Nehemiah Dibble—the very house that had served as General Tryon's headquarters during his brief occupation of Danbury.[19] One of the physicians attending the dying man was the enterprising Doctor Isaac Foster, who wrote on May 1, 1777.

> He [General Wooster] is in the same house with me, and I fear will not live until morning.[20]

The doctor was right. On Friday, May 2, 1777, General David Wooster died, and was buried the following Sunday in the cemetery bordering the street that was to bear his name.

AN EVALUATION OF GENERAL WOOSTER'S EFFORTS

These first two engagements are of some interest and importance to local history and legend, but to the British troops fighting the rear guard action that day, they were in no way distinguishable in the long running battle that was to ensue. In his report to Lord Germain, General Howe merely stated that "General Wooster hung upon the rear with a separate corps."[21] Robertson, who it will be remembered was with the British forces, barely alludes to the annoyance to the rear of the column. "They [Wooster's force] fired on the Rear at a great Distance with little harm." In making direct reference to Wooster, Robertson stated that "General Worcester [sic] at the same time attacked our Rear but was repulsed."[22]

While the British took little note of General Wooster's endeavors, and, indeed, the casualties he was able to inflict upon the retreating column were slight, Wooster succeeded in causing a delay in the arrival of the British at Ridgefield. This delay was sufficient to enable General Arnold to arrive ahead of the British and prepare for the defense of the village. His letter to McDougall of April 28 fixed the time of his arrival at Ridgefield at 11:00 A.M.[23]

General Arnold chose to make his stand at a naturally defensive position blocking the road leading to the village. With a force now numbering about 500 men, Arnold hastily erected a barricade of logs, stones, and carts across a narrow point in the road.[24] On the right of the barricade, as viewed from the American position, was the home and barn of Benjamin Stebbins. Beyond the house, the land dropped precipitously which protected the American right flank. On the American left flank, the ground rose to form a rocky ledge. Some 200 men were posted at the barricade while the remainder of the force protected the flanks.[25]

"We immediately (2 o'clock) Attack'd the Village and drove them off and took Possession."[26] With this terse description, Robertson described "the third and chief engagement of the Battle of Ridgefield."[27]

Traditional accounts from state and local histories are far more generous in their descriptions of this engagement than was Robertson, but, as is frequently the case, they lack credible documentation. These accounts, with varying degrees of elaboration, stem from the *Connecticut Journal* account of April 30, 1777. Here, the engagement is described as beginning with

> the approach of the enemy, who were soon discovered advancing in a column with three field pieces in front, and three in rear, and large flank guards of near two hundred men in each.—At noon they began discharging their artillery, and were soon within musket shot, when a smart action ensued between the whole, which continued about an hour, in which our men behaved with great spirit, but being overpowered by numbers, were obliged to give way, tho' not until the enemy were raising a small breast work, thrown across the way, at which Gen. Arnold had taken post with about 200 men (the rest of our small body were posted on the flanks) who acted with great spirit; the General Arnold had his horse shot under him, when the enemy were within about ten yards of him, but luckily received no hurt, recovering himself he drew his pistols and shot the soldier who was advancing with his fixed bayonet.—He then ordered his troops to retreat thro' a shower of small, and grape shot.[28]

Later historians have taken this account and embellished it with varying degrees of romanticism. These make for interesting and colorful reading, but they cannot be depended upon for the accuracy of the information they contain. Arnold himself described it as "a smart action which lasted about one hour."[29]

We have, then, described the three phases or engagements that are known as the *Battle of Ridgefield*. The *Connecticut Journal* of April 30 goes on to tell us that "It was found impossible to rally our troops, and Gen. Arnold ordered a stand to be made at Sagatuck [sic] bridge, where it was expected the enemy would pass."[30] The order to make the stand at the "Sagatuck bridge" is also supported in Arnold's own words.[31]

Based upon this information, the old accounts would lead us to believe that after the storming of the barricade (some versions tell us it was flanked), the British had uncontested control of Ridgefield, as the Americans retreated to new defensive positions at the Saugatuck bridge.

FURTHER SKIRMISHES FOR CONTROL OF RIDGEFIELD

There is sufficient documentary and physical evidence to support the contention that even after Arnold's defensive position was carried by the British, the Americans continued to fight for control of the village. In contrast to the lack of regard Robertson attached to the three engagements related above, he devoted considerable space in his journal to the actions *following* the third engagement. Robertson stated that

> after being in the Village a little while the Rebels again drew together and came up to gain a Rising Ground above the Village, upon which Sir William Erskine made a disposition to surround them. However by the different Companys not advancing at the same time, we only Dispersed them and drove them off. In three severe Skirmishes we had about 50 or 60 men Killed and Wounded and 4 or 5 Officers, Major (Henry) Hope, Capt. Rutherford, etc.[32]

In addition to Robertson's account, the number of cannonballs found in the village (in contrast to Danbury) is further evidence that the Americans continued to skirmish with and harass the British in the village itself.[33] The most famous of these cannonballs is lodged in the wall of the Keeler Tavern which is located at the south end of the village. This memento of the battle can be seen as part of a tour through this beautifully-preserved historic landmark.

The "three severe Skirmishes" described by Robertson would seem to allude to actions in the village itself. What is now popularly referred to as the first and second engagements should properly be referred to as the harassment of the British rear, distinguished only by the gallantry of General Wooster and the valuable delay his efforts achieved.

It is probable that another incident took place during the storming of Ridgefield by the British that was to contribute to one of the many inaccuracies found in the old accounts.

As we have seen, General Agnew was second-in-command of the expedition, and yet his name is scarcely to be found in any of the official records, and throughout the entire action, it was General Sir William Erskine who played the dominant role. This has probably led many historians to assume that General Erskine was the second-in-command.

A letter from one Alexander Andrew, servant to General Agnew, to Agnew's widow, following the general's death at the Battle of Germantown, sheds some light on the confusion regarding Agnew's proper role:

> Philadelphia   March 8, 1778
> On the expedition to Danberry [sic] the general was knocked down by a ball which left its mark for about a month.[34]

This mystery is, perhaps, explained: General Agnew was wounded, and, therefore, unable to actively lead the men, this role falling to the 3rd-in-command, Sir William Erskine. We cannot fix with any degree of certainty the exact action in which General Agnew received his wound, but we might reasonably conclude that it took place in the attack on Ridgefield, probably in the initial assault on Arnold's hastily-prepared defensive position. Some accounts say that it was General Agnew who led the flanking movement on Arnold's position.

General Agnew is not listed as one of the wounded officers in Howe's casualty report or enclosure to his dispatch No. 56 of 22/5/1777.[35] Again, we are left with a mystery concerning Tryon's second-in-command.

DAMAGE TO RIDGEFIELD

Although the village of Ridgefield contained no government stores, there was some destruction of private property. As in the case of Danbury, contemporary accounts do not reveal what proportion of the damage can be legitimately ascribed to the military action and what proportion was the result of arson or vandalism on the part of the British or American forces.

In his petition to the General Assembly seeking redress for losses, Philip B. Bradley stated that his losses were inflicted

> . . . either from the hand of the enemy or other persons ever ready to take advantages of such times of Distress and Confusion. That as the Enemy retreated thro the town of Ridgefield near the memorialist's dwelling House, where an action insued between them and the militia, in which the memoralist was also engaged, the M—— was obliged, and actually did deliver out of his own property about one hundred and twenty gallons of rum for the refreshment of the troops.[36]

If we allot one pint of rum per man, simple arithmetic will show that one hundred and twenty gallons would have been sufficient to "refresh" about 960 men. This figure more than exceeds the estimated American force in Ridgefield.

Perhaps the "revolutionary soldier" who gave such a glowing account of drunken disorder to Hollister (described above) was essentially correct; he just could not remember where it took place.

A memorial was submitted to the General Assembly by the Selectmen of Ridgefield on May 26, 1777. As in the case of Danbury, the purpose of the memorial was to obtain compensation. In part, it reads:

> That the Enemy, in their late incursion to Danbury on their return through Ridgefield and, burnt the Gristmill & Saw Mill of Mr Isaac Keeler of s^d Ridgefield, six dwelling houses two barnes [sic] and killed and carried off a number of horses, & Cattle, and on then Army took up their quarters in that Town for a Night, they plundered the inhabitants of almost all their Provisions and of a great part of their clothing, etc.[37]

The same committee that investigated the claims made by the grieved citizens of Danbury also visited Ridgefield for the same purpose. It is interesting too, that, in contrast to the nineteen claims submitted by Danbury residents, sixty-five claims were made by the citizens of Ridgefield. Seven of these claims were for sizeable amounts, representing the loss of the mill and the six homes. The remaining claims were for much smaller amounts and probably represent battle damage and the provisions taken by the troops. We may wonder what the troops did with all the civilian clothing they were accused of stealing.

BRITISH BIVOUAC IN RIDGEFIELD

As a result of the harassment to their rear and the "three severe Skirmishes" they fought, the British were able to march only ten miles on the first day of their retreat from Danbury.[38] They made camp that night (Sunday, April 27) a short distance south of the village on the road to Wilton. Robertson described the encampment: "We lay near the Village all night, four Battalions [Regiments] in line and two on the Wings, i.e. one on each wing."[39] There is no indication that the Americans attempted to harass the camp. In all probility, they were hurrying southward under Arnold to prepare new defensive positions.

GENERAL MCDOUGALL'S ATTEMPT TO INTERCEPT

The British broke camp at daybreak (5:01 A.M.) on the morning of April 28, and began the eighteen-mile march to the safety of the ships. "For five or six miles had only a few Popping Shots from behind houses Rocks etc."[40] This annoying fire undoubtedly came from the country people, as there is no indication from contemporary records of an organized harassment by the militia under either Arnold or Huntington.

While the British force had been resting on their arms Sunday night, General McDougall and his 1,200 men were making a difficult forced march from Peekskill to Bedford. In a letter to General Washington, General McDougall reported on his movements the night of April 27:

Peekskill, 29 April, 1 P.M., 1777

Sir,

I march'd, at 10 at night, [April 27] with about twelve hundred, and one Field-piece, towards Bedford, in hopes to fall in with the enemy there, from the intelligence contained in Number Eight of the inclosure [Arnold's letter]. At ten the next morning, I arrived at the south end of the town, at the road leading from Ridgefield, which is ten miles from Bedford. I had but just arrived there, when two ex-presses came in, and informed me that the enemy had left Ridgefield that morning at daybreak and marched towards Norwalk, which is but seventeen miles from the former; and that they had met with no opposition all morning. This intelligence deprived me of all hopes of coming up with them, in that distance, as they had rested at Ridgefield the night before, and we had marched twenty-one miles through very rough ground, without sleep or refreshment.[41]

The decision not to continue the pursuit of the retreating British column was not that of General McDougall alone. He called a Council of War to decide an issue that involved several considerations.

At a Council of war called at Bedford at 12 o'clock
on Monday the 28 instant—by order of Gen'l McDougal.

Officers Present.

Gen'l McDougall	Brig. Gen. Wolcolt
Col. Cortland	Col. Hooker
Lt. Col. Regnier	Lt. Col. Meade
Lt. Col. Porter	Lt. Col. Smith
Major Sumner	Major Ledyard
Major Sedgwick	Major Grey
Major Stanley	Major Brown

Gen'l McDougall having the moment before received
Intelligence by Express that the Enemy march from
Richfield [sic] at 2 o'clock A.M. the same day,
being at that time only seventeen Miles distant
from their shipping and having acquainted the
officers made the following motion, vis whether
it would be most prudent to pursue the enemy or
to return to Peeks Hill—

The Officers all (except Lt. Col. Smith and Maj. Sedgwick) unanimously agreed that it was more prudent to return to Peeks Hill, than to pursue enemy, from the two following considerations, vis, the exposed state of Peeks Hill and the great improbability of coming up with them.[42]

DESTRUCTION OF STORES IN WILTON

As the British column neared Wilton, they "Were inform'd [that] they [Americans] intended to oppose us at Norwalk Bridge. However by a clever move to our left we pass'd Another Bridge and got by them. Here we found Rum and other Stores in the Woods."[43] A return of those stores destroyed is by Robertson from his journal as follows:

> At the Bridge over the Norwalk River And in the woods adjacent
> 50 Hogsheads of Rum
> Some chests of Arms
> Paper Cartridges, Matches, Iron Forge, Bellows, etc.
> and a Number of Tents.[44]

Howe, in his report to Lord Germain, again embellished Robertson's report to read:

> At the bridge over the West branche of Norwalk River and in the woods contingent—
> 100 hogsheads of rum: several chests of arms: paper cartridges: field Forges: 300 Tents.[45]

There is little reason to believe that any organized stand had been planned by General Arnold at Norwalk Bridge. The only contemporary evidence concerning stores destroyed at Wilton seems to be a long memorial to the State Assembly for a receipt concerning "Ten hogshead of Rum destroyed in the month of April, 1777," by the troops of his Britannic Majesty "on their Rout [sic] to Danbury."

As Wilton was not on the *Route to* Danbury we are left to wonder if the memorialists, Eliakim Raymond and Lemuel Brooks, meant to say *"Rout from—."*[46]

GENERAL ARNOLD'S STAND AT SAUGATUCK BRIDGE

The present road from Wilton runs south for about ¾ mile where it branches to the east (Route 33); the main road (Route 7) continues to Norwalk.[47] The British forces took the road to Westport on the last leg of their march to the safety of their shipping.

In order to reach the embarkation point at Compo Beach, the British had to cross the Saugatuck River.[48] The most feasible means of crossing the river was to use the existing bridge. It was near this point that General Arnold had planned to make his stand.

Arnold's position was some distance above the bridge. His force had, by now, been augmented by the addition of some artillery pieces under the command of Lieutenant Colonel Eleazer Oswald. With regard to the size of Arnold's force, we are again at a loss to give an accurate figure. Kemble tells us that "Mr. Arnold, —lay in their way with a Body of near fifteen hundred Men.[49] Robertson, who has given us a precise account so far, says: "The Rebels appeared to me to be upwards of 4,000 men."[50] As we have seen before, British estimates of General Arnold's strength are widely exaggerated. Kemble's is a second-hand account, and Robertson's good judgment may have been impaired by the fatigue and strain of those last few hours. In reality, Arnold's strength appears to have been far less.

One of the accounts that provides us with a figure of Arnold's strength as he prepared to contest the crossing of the bridge comes to us from Colonel Hugh Hughes.[51] In a letter, dated "Monday 28 April 1777, Saugatuck Bridge 9 O'Clock," and addressed "Dear General [McDougall-Gates?]," Hughes related a series of events that day with several notations of time. At sometime following noon, ". . . there are about 300 men; and more coming constantly. Gen. Silliman is also here." At "1 O'Clock P.M.," Hughes continued: "I did myself the honor to wait on General Arnold, who made the best disposition of his little army on an advantageous situation."[52]

In a longer letter to General Gates, dated 3 May 1777, Fishkill, Hughes related to his superior officer a full account of the raid. In this letter, Hughes recalled Arnold's strength (at the breastworks) at "but 250 men and the enemy just in sight."[53]

Arnold described his force at "500 militia," and, as he put it, "at the beginning of the action Col. Huntington joined me with 500 men and before it was over a small number of Gen. Wadsworth's brigade."[54]

General Arnold's intentions were obvious to the British. Robertson stated that

> When we got within 5 miles of the Shore we got upon a high hill call'd Chestnut Hill, from which we could discern our Ships and the Rebels drawn up about 2 miles in front to oppose our Passing a Bridge over Sauketuck [sic] River.[55]

While General Arnold's force might have been small in numbers, it was a definite threat to the British retreat by reason of a six pounder provided by Colonel John Lamb's artillery company. The situation was similar, in some respects, to Arnold's stand at Ridgefield. The six pounder, and perhaps the sense of an impending disaster, caused the British to change their tactics. This time, there would be no assault.

60

We can measure the effect of Colonel Lamb's artillery in the words of Hughes:

> As soon as they were within reach of a six-pounder-he [Arnold] ordered a shot to be thrown among them which halted the whole first division, and the second [shot] put them into some disorder as it overset some of them. On which when the second division came up, it was determined by them to take a left hand road which led over a fording place at Saugatuck river. . . .[56]

To meet this challenge, Erskine made a show of force to the front and then wheeled to his left, crossing the river at a shallow ford.[57] To prevent General Arnold from crossing the bridge and striking their flank, two Regiments were pushed forward "to the Bridge by which means the Rebels were shut in untill all our Detachment pass'd by them in sight. Mr. Arnold endeavored to pass the Bridge but was not followed by his men."[58]

The failure of Arnold's militia to respond to his commands, both here at the bridge and in later actions at Compo Hill, provide colorful accounts of the American commander's relationship with these raw militia. Arnold himself best sums up his feelings towards the militia in his report to General McDougall: "Many of the officers behaved well—The Militia, *as usual*—[Arnold's underline] I wish never to see another of them in action."[59] Arnold's language might best be left to the imagination of the reader.

BRITISH MARCH TO SAFETY OF COMPO HILL

The 4th Regiment was left to hold the bridge, while the remainder of the British force began a rapid march to the beach.[60] The pace of the march and the rigors of the past few days were beginning to take their toll on British troops, as several of them dropped in the road with fatigue.[61]

At 1:00 P.M., the retreating troops were seen from the ships, and orders were given to prepare the flatboats for the embarkation. The day before (April 27), both *Senegal* and *Swan* had moved in closer to support the troops, and the transports were readied to receive the men.[62] *Swan* dispatched a petty officer and ten men on board an armed sloop to cover the embarkation.[63]

Once the entire British force had passed the bridge, the 4th Regiment, "being call'd off, we march'd from hill to hill towards the water side, the Rebels pressing on our Rear and Appearing in Considerable Numbers."[64] So pressing was the American attack on the British column that the 4th Regiment, now bringing up the rear, was nearly cut off.[65]

Despite the intensity with which the Americans harassed the

weary British troops, the British Advanced Guard occupied the heights of Compo Hill, with the remainder following close behind. "The rebels appearing on an eminence further back, began to cannonade."[66]

BATTLE OF COMPO HILL

The pressure of the American attack on Compo Hill forced the British back from two successive defensive positions behind stone walls. The situation, for them, was growing critical, as they had completely expended their ammunition. From *Senegal's* log we learn that she "Supplied the Army with 1,000 rounds of musket cartridges, theirs being expended."[67]

Without ammunition and in danger of being overwhelmed, the British ordered a charge with fixed bayonets. This assault was made by four Regiments: the 4th, 15th, 23rd, and 27th.[68] Kemple tells us that "the 4th and 15th Regiments principally, dashed over the Stone Wall and drove the Rebels with considerable loss."[69] Captain Hutchinson, in his long report to Lord Percy, related an incident of personal heroism as told to him by General Agnew and Agnew's Major of Brigade, Major Lesslie:

> [Major] Stewart, with about ten or twelve men only, rushed forward into the enemy's line and by his example, animated the rest of our troops to make a general charge, which by that time was become absolutely necessary from a want of ammunition, &c.[70]

THE EMBARKATION

This assault with the bayonet so demoralized the American forces that no further attempt was made to dislodge the British, despite the efforts of General Arnold to rally the militia for a further effort. As Robertson reported, "After this they never advanced more and we embarked on board our ships without a Shot being fired. Our men very much fatigued by so rapid and long a march."[71]

The embarkation began at 4:00 P.M. and continued undisturbed until all the troops, field pieces, and equipment were taken aboard the transports. The *Swan* received aboard the Provost and fifty-three prisoners of war.[72] By 7:30 P.M., the embarkation had been completed and the ships weighed anchor. Dropping out to five fathoms, they anchored again. At 9:00 P.M., *Senegal* made the signal for weighing, and at 9:30 P.M. the fleet set sail across the Sound, where the vessels anchored for the remainder of the night four miles SE of Oak Neck.[73]

MISINFORMATION CONCERNING RELIEF FORCE

Based upon the description given in the *Connecticut Journal* for

April 30, most accounts of the final battle at Compo Hill tell us that the British were saved from defeat by the timely arrival of a fresh relief force from the ships. This incorrect assumption rests upon two statements made in the *Connecticut Journal* and elaborated upon by successive historians. The two statements are: (1) "The enemy landed a number of fresh troops to cover their embarkation," and (2) "The enemy, the day before they left Fairfield [now Westport] were joined by ten sail, chiefly small vessels."[74]

Some writers would have us believe that a reserve force had been kept aboard for just such a contingency, or that the "10 sail" brought reinforcements from New York. Some historians, like Grumman, tell us that the relief force was composed of Royal Marines.[75] This myth of the Royal Marines saving the day is voiced by the reputable British historian, Sir George Trevelyn.[76]

Many comparisons can be made between the British efforts at Concord and Danbury, but not with regard to the efforts of a relief column. Unlike Colonel Smith's force at Concord, General Tryon's men had to extricate *themselves* from their precarious position because there was no relief force. It is true that the ship's heavy guns supported the embarkation and that some ammunition was supplied to the beleaguered force ashore, but the documentary evidence (particularly the ship's logs) clearly show that the entire force was committed at the time of the initial landing. No reserve was kept aboard; there were no Royal Marines.

With regard to the "10 sail" that figure so prominently in many accounts, we can turn again to the ships' logs for the answer. *Senegal's* log reads:

Sunday 27/4/1777
[Extract]   Saw 7 sail of schooner & sloops in the Sound, sent the pinnace on board them. The small vessels anchored S.E. of us.

Monday 28/4/1777:
[Extract]   At 3 P.M. anchored by us 7 *forage vessels*[77] from Huntington [Long Island].

The "10 sail," then, were forage ships and their escorts, and not reinforcements from New York.

RETURN TO NEW YORK

Weighing anchor at 5:00 A.M., Tuesday, April 29, the fleet proceeded down the Sound on its uneventful passage to New York. By 11:00 P.M., on Wednesday, April 30, the fleet had arrived at its anchorage off the Brothers Islands. All that remained was the debarkation of the troops. The details of the debarkation are best told in language of the ships' logs:

Senegal Thursday 1 May, 1777:

[Extract] 2 pm the 1st Division of troops disembarked for Harlem. At 4 (pm) the Generals, Capt. Duncan, and their retinue went for [New] York.—embarked the 2nd Division of troops for [New] York. Sent Captain Lymond (the wounded officer to Flushing) [British Hospital] in the pinnace.[78]

The provincial troops of Browne's Corps were not landed at Oyster Bay but were returned to New York with the British regular troops.[79] In his letter of May 31 to Lord Germain, Browne reported: "My Corps are all encamped at Kingsbridge."[80]

On Thursday, May 1, 1777, the *Swan* discharged the fifty-three prisoners taken during the raid. The British expedition to destroy the magazine at Danbury had been concluded.

Conclusions

Any assessment of the British raid on Danbury, Connecticut, must consider the immediate results and the effects of the raid upon the larger conflict. This account leaves no doubt that the British were eminently successful in achieving their immediate objective. It is true that the raid was not stategic, but to suggest that its results were limited to the destruction of the stores is to ignore several important consequences of those events. If the raid on Danbury deserves a place in the history of the Revolutionary War, it should be for its influence upon later events, rather than for its immediate tactical value.

The loss of the stores was hard for the Americans to bear, but in no respect did it affect the campaign of 1777. Shortages of all sorts— food, clothing, munitions, and men—were items of daily concern throughout the entire war. The loss of these stores appears to have been but one more headache for the overburdened procurement service of the American Army.

The tents were the only material that could not be raised or produced locally to replace that which had been destroyed. This was admitted by General Washington to be the "chief loss we sustained."[1] Britain's economic policy had left the Americans without an industrial base with which to replace this item. Replacements for the destroyed tents would have to come from France.

The disposition of a shipment of tents from France was to provoke a bitter controversy between General Gates of the Northern Department and General Washington.[2] This exchange of letters undoubtedly affected the relationship between these two men, and, in particular, the role that General Gates was to play in the remaining years of the war.

The most far-reaching result of the British raid on Danbury could be said to be the influence it had upon the career of Benedict Arnold, and, in turn, his contribution to the American effort. Arnold had become bitter in his feelings towards the Army and the Congress for their failure to reward him, through promotion, for his contributions to the American cause. Many historians feel that he might well have resigned his commission.[3]

Following the raid, Arnold received his belated promotion from Congress for his heroic efforts at Ridgefield and Compo. A fully-caparisoned horse was also given to the 'hero of the day" by Congress, apparently attempting to correct its earlier slight of Arnold.[4] The promotion left Arnold still junior to those who had been promoted over him. Despite the recognition bestowed upon him, Arnold felt that his honor had not been entirely vindicated. Conciliatory letters from General Washington, however, had the effect of placating Arnold, and he went (not wholly satisfied) to his next assignment as second in command to General Gates, who had the problem of dealing with General Burgoyne preparing to advance down from Canada.[5]

If we accept the theory advanced by most historians of the Revolution, that it was Arnold's courage, skill, and enterprise that won the day at Saratoga, then it must follow that the British Raid on Danbury had far-reaching implications. As all students of this period know, the Battle of Saratoga is generally credited with being "the decisive battle of the war," in that it caused the French to participate actively as an ally of the Americans.

One can conclude, then, that the British raid on Danbury enabled Arnold to win the recognition he needed to remain in the army. This placed him in a position to make an invaluable contribution to the American cause.

The inability of the Americans to protect Danbury and the subsequent loss of the stores came at an unfortunate moment. At that time (April, 1777, six months prior to Saratoga), the French government was attempting to evaluate the military capabilities of the Americans. France was, even then, considering entering the conflict on the side of the Americans. In order to ascertain the true state of affairs, the Chevalier D'Anmours had come to America to determine the military and political situations within the colonies, and report back to Paris. His observations following the raid on Danbury were so detrimental to American interests that General Washington addressed a long letter to the Chevalier in order to correct any misconceptions concerning the Americans' ability and willingness to continue the war:

[Excerpt] Permit me, Sir, to correct a mistake you made, in narrating a fact, with respect to the Danbury expedition, in which some Magazines of ours were destroyed. You mention only an hundred Men, being lost to the Enemy; but from various accounts and circumstances, there is little reason to doubt there must have been at least four hundred killed, wounded and taken. I have taken notice of this error, because it is of some little importance, the affair should be rightly stated, as it serves to show in a stricking point of view, the spirit of opposition prevailing among the people, which animated them to Assemble on so sudden an occasion, and to attack a regular Body of two thousand Men, with so much Vigor, as to force them to a precipitate return, little differing from a rout.[6]

British ability to operate deep within American lines and to destroy a sizeable amount of stores was demonstrated at a critical time in French-American relations. One can imagine how the news was received by Benjamin Franklin and the other American commissioners working so diligently to convince the French Government of the advisability of participating with America against the British.

The lessons of the raid were not lost on either the British or American commanders-in-chief. For the Americans, it was the realization that they lacked the manpower to protect every post and town laid open to attack as a result of the great mobility of the enemy through their control of the sea. In letters to Brigadier General Parsons (May 7) and to Governor Trumbull of Connecticut (May 11), General Washington attempted to justify his strategy of collecting all available manpower in New Jersey to protect the Hudson Highlands and Philadelphia. He stated

. . . that the Enemy will harrass [sic] our Coasts and injure the maritime Towns, with their shipping and by sudden debarkations of small parties of Men, is not improbable and what we cannot prevent, whilst they have the entire command of the Water—I should be happy, were it in my power, to station Guards of Continental Troops at every Place, subject to the depredations of the Enemy; but this cannot be done. If we divide and detach our Forces to every part, where the Enemy may possibly attempt an impression, we shall effect no one good purpose, and in the end, destroy ourselves and subjugate our Country.[7]

As suitable forces to protect the depots in Connecticut could not be spared, the stores were moved further inland. Danbury continued to be used as a military depot, but additional measures were taken to protect it against a recurring attack. Several brigades under General Putnam were quartered for the winter (1777-78) in Redding. The following winter, several other brigades were quartered southeast of Danbury in the Shelter Rock area. These troops were to provide the necessary protection should the British attempt to repeat the raid of April, 1777.

The British learned that, while their control of the sea gave them great mobility, they could not venture inland with impunity. General Clinton, in reference to Lord Cornwallis' detachment of troops in one of the southern campaigns (Kings Mountain), stated:

> It is, however, a matter much to be lamented that during the whole of His Lordship's [Cornwallis] command he was certainly too apt to risk detachments without proper support, which is more to be wondered at as Lexington, Bennington, Danbury and Trenton were recent instances which His Lordship could not have forgot.[8]

It is clear that, privately, some British generals considered the raid on Danbury in the light of a defeat. While the British raided the coast of Connecticut and other northern maritime states throughout the war, they never attempted to penetrate inland, but contented themselves with the destruction of coastal facilities.

The British raid on Danbury was not a major battle, but it did have a surprisingly large impact on the subsequent events of the war. The lives and careers of several men were affected, as was local legend and history. To a certain extent, both armies maneuvered in accordance with the lessons learned. The raid on Danbury deserves its place in any extensive history of the Revolutionary War because circumstances made the raid possible and, in turn, the raid was to influence and color later events of the conflict.

Notes

THE CAUSES OF AND CONTRIBUTORY FACTORS TO THE BRITISH RAID ON DANBURY

1. R. Ernest DuPuy and Trevor N. DuPuy, *The Compact History of the Revolutionary War* (New York: Hawthorn Books Co., 1963), p. 159.

2. John Richard Alden, *The American Revolution* (New York: Harper and Brothers, 1954), p. 121.

3. DuPuy and DuPuy, *op. cit.*, p. 221.

4. A. T. Mahan, *The Major Operations of the Navies in the War of American Independence* (Boston: Little, Brown and Co., 1913), p. 57.

5. Alden, *op. cit.*, pp. 112-118.

6. *The Narrative of Lieut. Gen. Sir William Howe*, 3rd. Ed. (London: H. Baldwin, 1781), p. 9.

7. Peter Force, ed., *American Archives*, Fifth Series (Washington: 1848-1853), III, 1318.

8. *Ibid.*

9. *Narrative of Howe*, p. 12. Italics mine.

10. Alden, *op. cit.*, p. 116.

11. *Ibid.*, p. 115.

12. William B. Wilcox, *Protrait of a General* (New York: Alfred A. Knopf, 1964), p. 143.

13. *Ibid.*

14. Alden, *op. cit.,* p. 118.

15. Jared Sparks, *The Life of Washington* (Boston: Tappan, Whittmore, and Mason, 1849), p. 228.

16. DuPuy and DuPuy, *op. cit.,* p. 189.

17. Sparks, *loc. cit.*

18. Force, *op. cit.,* III, 1337.

19. *Ibid.,* III, 1446.

20. *Ibid.,* III, 1465.

21. *Ibid.,* III, 1465.

22. *Ibid.,* III, 1469.

23. National Archives, Record Group 360, Item IV, Folio 129.

24. Trumbull Papers, Connecticut Historical Society, Hartford, Connecticut.

25. Alden, *op. cit.,* p. 115.

26. William T. Horton, *A History of Peekskill, New York* (Peekskill: The Enterprise Press, 1954), p. 49.

27. Christopher Ward, *The War of the Revolution* (2 vols.; New York: The MacMillan Co., 1952), I, 323.

28. Edward E. Curtis, *The Organization of the British Army in the American Revolution* (New York: Yale University Press, 1926), p. 102.

29. Ward, *op. cit.,* p. 401.

30. Force, *op. cit.,* III, 1318.

31. Charles Stedman, *The History . . . of the American War* (2 vols.; Dublin: Wogan, Byrne, Moon, Jones, 1794), I, 312.

32. DuPuy and DuPuy, *op. cit.,* p. 147.

33. Ward, *op. cit.,* I, 240.

34. *Ibid.,* p. 322.

35. DuPuy and DuPuy, *op. cit.,* p. 186.

36. Ward, *op. cit.,* I, 322.

37. Alden, *op. cit.,* p. 119.

38. Emma L. Patterson, *Peekskill in the American Revolution* (Peekskill: Highland Democrat Co., 1944), p. 80.

39. Horton, *op. cit.,* p. 48.

40. Patterson, *op. cit.,* p. 43.

41. Curtis, *op. cit.,* p. 102.

42. Ward, *op. cit.,* II, 659.

43. *Ibid.*

44. Carl Van Doren, *Secret History of the American Revolution* (New York: The Viking Press, 1941), p. 28.

45. *Ibid.*

46. DuPuy and DuPuy, *op. cit.,* p. 121.

47. Stedman, *op. cit.,* I, 312.

48. Force, *op. cit.,* III, 1514.

49. Ward, *op. cit.,* I, 286.

50. George F. Scheer and Hugh F. Rankin, *Rebels and Redcoats* (New York: The World Publishing Co., 1957), p. 225.

THE ORGANIZATION AND COMPOSITION OF THE BRITISH EXPEDITIONARY FORCE

1. E. B. O'Callaghan, *Documents Relative to the History of the State of New York* (Albany, 1852), VIII, 713. Italics mine.

2. *Ibid.*

3. Mark Mayo Boatner, III, *Encyclopedia of the American Revolution* (New York: David McKay Co., 1966), p. 560.

4. Orderly Book of British Headquarters, Feb. 14, 1777-June 2, 1777 kept by Capt. Knight, Aide de Camp to Commander in Chief. New York Historical Society, N. Y. C.

5. O'Callaghan, *op. cit.*, VIII, 706.

6. *Ibid.*

7. William Edgar Grumman, *The Revolutionary Soldiers of Redding, Connecticut* (Hartford: The Case, Lockwood, and Brainard Co., 1904), p. 38.

8. *Journal of Col. Stephen Kemble* (New York Historical Society, 1884), p. 113. Kemble's figure of 200 is incorrect.

9. *Archibald Robertson—His Diaries and Sketches in America 1767-1780* (New York Public Library, 1930).

10. Alden, *op. cit.*, p. 270, nl.

11. Robertson, *op. cit.*, p. 126.

12. Ward, *op. cit.*, I, 47.

13. Robertson, *loc. cit.*

14. Alden, *op. cit.*, p. 224.

15. Charles M. Lefferts, *Uniforms of the American, British, French, German Armies in the War of the American Revolution* (New York: New York Historical Society, 1926).

16. Ward, *op. cit.*, I, 260.

17. *New York Gazette and Weekly Mercury*, March 3, 1777.

18. Grumman, *op. cit.*, p. 43.

19. *An American's Experience in the British Army* by Col. Stephen Jarvis, *Journal of American History*, I (Third quarter, 1907), p. 446.

20. *Ibid.*

21. Robertson, *loc. cit.*

22. Admiralty Records, London, 51/960, Part 3. Hereafter cited as Adm. with proper sub-identification.

23. Colonial Office, London, 5/94 f179. Hereafter cited as CO. with proper sub-identification.

24. Robertson, *loc. cit.*

25. Letter from Major R. St. G. G. Bartelot, Royal Artillery Institution, Feb. 7, 1968.

26. Grumman, *op. cit.*, p. 52. Capt. Hutchinson, Aide de Camp to Lord Percy, was a passenger on board the packet *Mercury* making its way down the Sound when she came upon the embarkation of the British troops. He went aboard *Senegal* to gather information for Lord Percy.

27. *Ibid.*

28. Adm. 51/960, Part 3.

29. William Hanford Burr, "The Invasion of Connecticut by the British," *Connecticut Magazine* (1906), p. 146.

30. Wilcox, *op. cit.*, p. 99.

31. Adm. 1/487 f361.

32.. Adm. 1/487 f375.

33. Adm. 1/487 f361.

34. Kemble, *op. cit.*, p. 113.

35. Horton, *op. cit.*, p. 49.

THE PROGRESS OF THE EXPEDITION TO DANBURY

1. Robertson, *op. cit.*, p. 126.
2. Adm. 52/1775 Part 2.

3. British Headquarters Papers, #10,216, New York Public Library [Photostat]. Original now at Public Record Office, London.

4. Kemble, *op. cit.*, p. 114.

5. DuPuy and DuPuy, *op. cit.*, p. 127.

6. Kemble, *loc. cit.*

7. Transports were not required to keep log books.

8. Officers commanding sloops were rated as Commanders, but were accorded the courtesy title of Captain.

9. Adm. 51/885.

10. Adm. 36/7769.

11. Adm. 51/885.

12. Adm. 51/960.

13. *Ibid.*

14. Adm. 51/885.

15. *Ibid.*

16. Adm. 51/1775.

17. Adm. 51/885.

18. Washington to Brigadier General Maxwell, April 17, 1777, in John C. Fitzpatrick, ed., *The Writings of George Washington* (New York: MacMillan Co., 1931-1944), VII, 416.

19. *Ibid.*, p. 431.

20. National Archives, Record Group 360, Item IV. Folio 99.

21. *Ibid.*, p. 459.

22. *Ibid.*, p. 466.

23. *Ibid.*, p. 474. Italics mine.

24. Royal R. Hinman, *A Historical Collection of the Part Sustained by Connecticut During the War of the Revolution* (Hartford: E. Gleason, 1842), p. 433.

25. *Ibid.*, p. 438.

26. Grumman, *op. cit.*, pp. 38-39.

27. Louis F. Middlebrook, *Maritime Connecticut During the American Revolution* (2 vols.; Salem, Mass.: The Essex Institute, 1925), I, 15.

28. Adm. 52/1775, Part 2.

29. During this period, British naval logs were kept from noon to noon.

30. Adm. 51/885. A spring is a mooring device consisting of two anchors and two cables that would enable an anchored vessel to maneuver and thus bring her guns to bear.

31. Grumman, *op. cit.*, pp. 39-40.

32. Adm. 51/885.

33. Robertson, *op. cit.*, pp. 126-127.

34. *Ibid.*

35. Adm. 52/1775, P/667/8.

36. *Ibid.*

37. Middlebrook, *op. cit.*, II, 242.

38. Hinman, *op. cit.*, p. 112.

39. National Archives, Record Group 360, Item IV, Folio 128.

40. Grumman, *op. cit.*, p. 44.

41. James Montgomery Bailey, *History of Danbury, Conn.* (New York: Burr Printing House, 1896), p. 61.

42. Robertson, *op. cit.*, p. 127.

43. Burr, *loc. cit.*

44. Robertson, *loc. cit.*

45. Adm. 51/885. Probably one of the now-empty transports served as a Hospital Ship.

46. Hinman, *op. cit.*, p. 120.

47. Grumman, *op. cit.*, p. 43.
48. Bailey, *loc. cit.*
49. *Ibid.*, p. 62.
50. Grumman, *op. cit.*, p. 44.
51. Robertson, *loc. cit.*
52. Charles Burr Todd, *The History of Redding, Conn.* (New York: The John A. Gray Press, 1880), p. 51.
53. (Philadelphia and New York: J. B. Lippincott, 1959).
54. *Ibid.*
55. Robertson, *loc. cit.*
56. *Ibid.*
57. Bailey, *op. cit.*, p. 66.
58. *Ibid.*
59. *Ibid.*, p. 62.
60. National Archives, Record Group 360, Item IV.

THE BRITISH OCCUPATION OF DANBURY

1. *Connecticut Journal*, April 23, 1777.
2. Worthington C. Ford, ed., *Correspondence and Journals of Samuel Blachley Webb* (Lancaster, Pa.: Wickersham Press, 1893), I, 205. Italics mine.
3. Fitzpatrick, *op. cit.*, VII, 459.
4. Douglas Southall Freeman, *George Washington* (New York: Charles Scribner's Sons, 1951) IV, 410.
5. John Marshall, *The Life of George Washington* (Fredericksburg, Va., 1926) II, 273.
6. Bailey, *op. cit.*, p. 65.
7. *Ibid.*, p. 30.
8. *Ibid.*, p. 62.
9. National Archives. Record Group 360, Item IV, Folio 129.
10. *Ibid.*
11. Bailey, *op. cit.*, p. 30.
12. *Ibid.*, p. 62.
13. *Ibid.*
14. Robertson, *op. cit.*, p. 127.
15. National Archives, Record Group 360, Item IV, Folio 137.
16. Bailey, *loc. cit.*
17. *Ibid.*, p. 68. Italics mine.
18. Robertson, *loc. cit.*
19. The correct title should read: *The Viscount Falkland.*
20. Hinman, *op. cit.*, p. 601.
21. *Ibid.*
22. Bailey, *op. cit.*, p. 68.
23. Connecticut Archives, Series I, Documents of the Revolution, State Library, Hartford, Connecticut, XXXVII, 229-231. See also David O. White, *Connecticut's Black Soldiers: 1775-1783* (Chester, Connecticut: Pequot Press, 1973), p. 28.
24. Hinman, *loc. cit.*
25. Ward, *op. cit.*, I, 48.
26. Allen French, ed., *A British Fusilier in Revolutionary Boston* (Boston: Harvard University Press, 1926), p. 56.
27. Benson J. Lossing, *Pictorial Field Book of the Revolution* (New York: Harper Bros., 1859), I, 403.
28. Bailey, *op. cit.*, p. 68.

29. Robertson, *loc. cit.*

30. CO 5/94, ff. 195-196. Italics mine.

31. Thomas Glyn, Ens., Journal On the American Service, Princeton University Library.

32. Grumman, *op. cit.*, p. 46.

33. Bailey, *op. cit.*, p. 61.

34. Lynn Montross, *Rag, Tag, and Bobtail* (New York: Harper Bros., 1952), p. 180.

35. National Archives, Record Group 360, Item IV, Folio 139.

36. Grumman, *loc. cit.*

37. Kemble, *op. cit.*, p. 116.

38. Hinman, *op. cit.*, p. 559.

39. *Ibid.*, p. 377.

40. Charles J. Hoadly, ed., *The Public Records of the State of Connecticut* (Hartford: 1894). p. 286.

41. Lossing, *op. cit.*, p. 404.

42. Kemble, *loc. cit.*

43. Bailey, *op. cit.*, p. 69.

44. G. H. Hollister, *The History of Connecticut* (2 vols. New Haven: Durrie and Peck, 1855), II, 300.

45. Lossing, *loc. cit.*

46. *The American Journal of Ambrose Serle* (San Marino, California: The Huntington Library, 1940), p. 217.

47. Knight, *loc. cit.*

48. Bailey, *op. cit.*, p. 72.

49. Hinman, *op. cit.*, p. 614.

50. *Ibid.*

51. Bailey, *op. cit.*, p. 55.

52. Burr, *loc. cit.*

53. Glynn, *loc. cit.*

54. Robertson, *loc. cit.*

55. Italics mine.

56. Hinman, *op. cit.*, pp. 118-119. Italics mine.

57. *Ibid.*

58. *Ibid.*

59. CO, 5/94 ff195-196.

60. Bailey, *op. cit.*, p. 83. Italics mine.

61. CO. 5/94 ff195-196.

62. CO 5/94 f198 [unsigned].

63. Robertson, *op. cit.*, pp. 129-130.

64. Kemble, *loc. cit.*

65. Glyn, *loc. cit.*

66. Glyn and Robertson use the rank of General in reference to Arnold, although many contemporary accounts refused this honor. In many accounts, the form of address used is *Mister*. This holds true not only of Arnold but with others, including Washington. In his despatch (No. 54) to Germain, Howe does refer to "General Arnold," but penciled in the margin is a note (obviously added in London), reading: "If this is inserted in the [London] Gazette, the title of General should be omitted."

67. Robertson, *loc. cit.*

68. National Archives, Record Group 360, Item IV, Folio 135.

1. National Archives, Record Group 360, Item IV, Folio 139.

2. Robertson, *op. cit.,* p. 127.

3. *Ibid.*

4. The American defenses guarding the Hudson Highlands consisted primarily of Fort Independence on the east bank, and Forts Clinton and Montgomery on the west bank.

5. McDougall Papers, New York Historical Society, New York, N.Y.

6. Jared Sparks, *Correspondence of the American Revolution* (Boston: Little, Brown, Co. 1853), I, 373-374.

7. National Archives, Record Group 360, Item IV, Folio 133.

8. Bailey, *op. cit.,* p. 76.

9. National Archives, Record Group 360, Item IV, Folio 125.

10. Silvio A. Bedini, *Ridgefield in Review* (The Ridgefield 250th Anniversary Committee, Inc., Ridgefield, Conn., 1958, printed by Walker-Rackliff, New Haven, Conn.), p. 77.

11. CO. 5/94 f198.

12. Robertson, *op. cit.,* p. 130.

13. CO. 5/94 f200 (Enclosure [signed] to Sir Wm. Howe's Dispatch No. 56, 22/5/1777).

14. *Connecticut Journal,* May 7, 1777.

15. National Archives, Record Group 360 Item IV, Folio 143.

16. Bedini, *op. cit.,* p. 66.

17. *Ibid.,* p. 67.

18. *Ibid.*

19. Bailey, *op. cit.,* p. 85.

20. *Ibid.,* p. 63.

21. CO. 5/94 ff195-196.

22. Robertson, *op. cit.,* p. 128.

23. National Archives, Record Group 360, Item IV, Folio 139.

24. *Ibid.*

25. *Connecticut Journal,* April 30, 1777.

26. Robertson, *loc. cit.*

27. From a State of Connecticut historic marker: *Battle of Ridgefield April 27, 1777 The Third and Chief Engagement Occurred on this Ridge.*

28. *Connecticut Journal, loc. cit.*

29. National Archives, Record Group 360, Item IV, Folio 139.

30. *Connecticut Journal, loc. cit.*

31. National Archives, Record Group 360, Item IV, Folio 139.

32. Robertson, *loc. cit.*

33. Bedini, *op. cit.,* p. 79.

34. Lossing, *op. cit.,* p. 319.

35. CO. 5/94 f200.

36. Series I, VII: 227, Records of the American Revolution, Connecticut State Library, Hartford.

37. Series I, VII: 28, Records of the American Revolution, State Library, Hartford.

38. Robertson, *loc. cit.*

39. *Ibid.*

40. *Ibid.*

41. National Archives, Record Group 360, Item IV, Folio 127.

42. McDougall Papers.

43. Robertson, *loc. cit.*

44. *Ibid.*

45. CO. 5/94 f198.

46. *The Public Records of the State of Connecticut 1783-84* (Hartford, 1894), pp. 466-467.

47. Today, Routes 33 and 7 are one and the same from their juncture to a point about ¾ of a mile south. Here, Route 33 branches to the east and Westport, while Route 7 continues south to Norwalk.

48. The road the British took (Route 33) lies on the west bank of the river; their shipping off Compo Beach was on the east side of the river mouth.

49. Kemble, *op. cit.*, p. 116.

50. Robertson, *op. cit.*, p. 129. At no time did the size of the American force equal or surpass that of the British.

51. Col. Hugh Hughes, Deputy Quarter Master General to Gen. Gates. Hughes was in the Danbury area on a mission to procure stores for the army of the Northern Department under Gen. Gates.

52. National Archives, Record Group 360, Item IV, Folio 141.

53. Gates Papers, N.Y. Historical Society.

54. National Archives, Record Group 360, Item IV, Folio 145.

55. Robertson, *op. cit.*, p. 128.

56. Gates Papers, *op. cit.*

57. Kemble, *loc. cit.*

58. Robertson, *op. cit.*, pp. 128-129.

59. National Archives, Record Group 360, Item IV, Folio 145.

60. Robertson, *op. cit.*, p. 129.

61. Stedman, *op. cit.*, p. 313.

62. Adm. 51/885.

63. Adm. 51/960, part 3.

64. Robertson, *op. cit.*, p. 129.

65. Kemble, *op. cit.*, p. 117.

66. Adm. 51/885.

67. *Ibid.*

68. Robertson, *loc. cit.*

69. Kemble, *loc. cit.*

70. Grumman, *op. cit.*, p. 52.

71. Robertson, *loc. cit.*

72. Adm. 51/960.

73. Adm. 51/885.

74. *Connecticut Journal, loc. cit.*

75. Grumman, *op. cit.*, p. 49.

76. Sir George Otto Trevelyan, *The American Revolution* (New York: Green and Co., 1907), Part III, p. 118.

77. Adm. 51/885. Italics mine. Because ship's logs were kept from 12 noon to 12 noon, both entries were actually within the same day as we reckon time.

78. Adm. 51/885.

79. Adm. 51/960, Part 3.

80. Grumman, *op. cit.*, p. 58.

CONCLUSIONS

1. Fitzpatrick, *op. cit.*, p. 158.

2. Freeman, *op. cit.*, p. 44.

3. DuPuy and DuPuy, *op. cit.*, p. 191.

4. Ward, *op. cit.*, p. 495.

5. *Ibid.*

6. Fitzpatrick, *op. cit.*, VIII, 266.

7. *Ibid.*, VIII, 42.

8. William B. Wilcox, ed., *Sir Henry Clinton's Narrative of His Campaigns 1775-1782* (New York, 1964), p. 227.

For Further Reading

Alden, John Richard. *The American Revolution*. New York: Harper and Brothers, 1954.

Anderson, Troyer S. *The Command of the Howe Brothers During the American Revolution*. New York: 1936.

Bailey, James Montgomery. *History of Danbury, Connecticut*. New York: Burr Printing House, 1896.

Bedini, Silvio A. *Ridgefield in Review*. New Haven: Walker-Rackliff, 1958.

Boatner, Mark Mayo, III. *Encyclopedia of the American Revolution*. New York: David McKay Co. Inc., 1966.

Curtis, Edward E. *The Organization of the British Army in the American Revolution*. New Haven: Yale University Press, 1926.

DuPuy, R. Ernest and Trevor N. DuPuy. *The Compact History of the Revolutionary War*. New York: Hawthorn Books Co., 1963.

Force, Peter (ed.). *American Archives*, Fifth Series Vol. III. Washington, 1848-1853.

Ford, Worthington C. (ed.). *Correspondence and Journals of Samuel Blachley Webb*. Lancaster, Pennsylvania: Wickersham Press, 1893.

Freeman, Douglas Southall. *George Washington*. New York: Charles Scribner's Sons, 1951.

French, Allen (ed.). *A British Fusilier in Revolutionary Boston*. Boston: Harvard University Press, 1926.

Grumman, William Edgar. *The Revolutionary Soldiers of Redding, Connecticut*. Hartford: The Case, Lockwood and Brainard Co., 1904.

Hinman, Royal R. *A Historical Collection of the Part Sustained by Connecticut During the War of the Revolution*. Hartford: E. Gleason, 1842.

Hollister, G. H. *The History of Connecticut*, 2 vols. New Haven: Durrie and Peck, 1855.

Hoadly, Charles J. *et al.* (eds.). *The Public Records of the State of Connecticut*. 11 vols., Hartford, 1894-1967.

Horton, William T. *A History of Peekskill, New York*. Peekskill: The Enterprise Press, 1964.

Howe, Sir William. *The Narrative of Lieutenant General Sir William Howe*, 3rd Edition. London: H. Baldwin, 1781.

Leiby, Andrian C. *The Revolutionary War in the Hackensack Valley*. New Brunswick, New Jersey: Rutgers University Press, 1962.

Lossing, Benson J. *Pictorial Field Book of the Revolution*. New York: Harper Bros., 1859.

Mahan, A. T. *The Major Operations of the Navies in the War of American Independence*. Boston: Little, Brown and Co., 1913.

Marshall, John. *The Life of George Washington* Vol. II. Fredericksburg, Virginia, 1926.

Middlebrook, Louis F. *Maritime Connecticut During the American Revolution.* 2 vols., Salem, Massachusetts: The Essex Institute, 1925.

Montross, Lynn. *Rag, Tag, and Bobtail.* New York: Harper Bros., 1952.

Patterson, Emma L. *Peekskill in the American Revolution.* Peekskill: Highland Democrat Co., 1944.

Scheer, George F. and Hugh F. Rankin. *Rebels and Redcoats.* New York: The World Publishing Co., 1957.

Stedman, Charles. *The History . . . of the American War.* 2 vols., Dublin: Wogan, Byrne, Moon, Jones, 1794.

Todd, Charles Burr. *The History of Redding, Connecticut.* New York: The John A. Gray Press, 1880.

Trevelyan, Sir George Otto. *The American Revolution,* Part III. New York: Green and Co., 1907.

Van Doran, Carl. *The Secret History of the American Revolution.* New York: The Viking Press, 1941.

Ward, Christopher. *The War of the Revolution.* 2 vols., New York: The MacMillan Co., 1952.

Wilcox, William B. *Portrait of a General.* New York: Alfred A. Knopf, 1964.

Wilcox, William B. (ed.). *Sir Henry Clinton's Narrative of His Campaigns, 1775-1782.* New Haven: Yale University Press, 1954.

Wilson, Lynn Winfield. *History of Fairfield County Connecticut.* Chicago-Hartford: S. J. Clarke Publishing Co., 1929.

PUBLISHED JOURNALS

Archibald Robertson. *His Diaries and Sketches in America 1767-1780.* New York: New York Public Library, 1930.

Journal of Colonel Stephen Kemble. New York Historical Society, 1884.

The American Journal of Ambrose Serle. San Marino, California: The Huntington Library, 1940.